The Hamlyn All-Colour

Garden Book

Introduced by Percy Thrower

Annual Pink
Dianthus

Site: sunny.

Soil: ordinary, well-drained.

Height: 15 to 30 cm (6 to 12 in).

Spread: 15 to 20 cm (6 to 8 in).

Type of plant: half-hardy annual.

Flowers: single or double flowers in shades of red, mauve, pink and white.

Flowering time: summer.

Sowing time: late winter to early spring (under glass, 13°C, 55°F), outdoors in frost-free climates.

Planting time: early summer, when danger of frost is past.

Planting distance: 15 to 23 cm (6 to 9 in).

Species cultivated: *D. chinensis* and its variety *heddewigii* are available in a number of brilliantly coloured varieties; among the best of these are: 'Queen of Hearts' 30 cm (12 in), single, red; 'Baby Doll Mixed' 15 cm (6 in), 'Brilliancy' (photograph) single, rich cerise-pink, 'Snowflake' 20 cm (8 in), single white.

Cultivation and uses: no special requirements; excellent plants for the front of a sunny border, or for planting in pockets on the rock garden; look particularly at home planted alongside paths.

Larkspur
Delphinium

Site: sunny.

Soil: ordinary, not too dry.

Height: 30 to 120 cm (1 to 4 ft).

Spread: 30 cm (1 ft).

Type of plant: hardy annual.

Flowers: tall spikes of white, pink, mauve, blue or purple.

Flowering time: summer.

Sowing time: spring (outdoors where plants are to flower; thin seedlings to 23 cm (9 in) when large enough to handle.

Species cultivated: *D. ajacis* is the parent of most annual varieties of larkspur; recommended varieties: 'White Spire' 121 cm (4 ft), (photograph), 'Blue Spire', 'White Spire', 'Hyacinth Flowered' 45 cm (18 in), mixed, relatively early flowering; many mixed varieties are available and these vary in height.

Cultivation and uses: stake taller varieties with twiggy branches; good plants for beds and borders where they can be positioned towards the back to give height to a display.

114

The Hamlyn All-Colour
Garden Book
Introduced by Percy Thrower
Photography by Rob Herwig

Foxglove
Digitalis

Star of the Veldt
Dimorphotheca

Fritillaria imperialis 'Lutea'

Hamlyn
London New York Sydney Toronto

Acknowledgements

Line drawings by Ron Hayward
Photographs of *Berberis thunbergii*, page 76, *Pyracantha
watereri*, page 80 by The Harry Smith Horticultural
Photographic Collection and *Ornithogalum*, page 136 by Valerie Finnis

The editor would like to thank L. R. Russell Ltd.
of Windlesham, Surrey for supplying
Magnolia kobus for the jacket photograph.

Plant information compiled by Barbara Haynes B.Sc (Hort Sci.)
Susanne Mitchell B.Sc (Hort) Alan Titchmarsh Dip. Hort. (Kew)

First published in 1979 by
The Hamlyn Publishing Group Limited
London · New York · Sydney · Toronto
Astronaut House, Feltham, Middlesex, England

© Copyright colour photographs Uitgeverij Het Spectrum B.V.,
Utrecht/Amsterdam, The Netherlands 1979
© Copyright text and line illustrations The Hamlyn Publishing
Group Limited 1979

Filmset in England by Tradespools Limited, Frome, Somerset
in 10 on 11pt Garamond

Printed in Italy
ISBN 0 600 34106 2

Contents

Introduction

Planting up a new garden or adding plants to an existing garden is the most rewarding of exercises, and one of which, I am glad to say, I have had plenty of experience. As a result of this there is one thing which I would stress more than any other and it is that you consider long and hard before giving space to trees, shrubs, conifers, herbaceous perennials and so on which are permanent, as opposed to transitory, plants.

If your choices are wise then nothing is more certain than that they will give you pleasure for many years to come; if unwise – either because they do not relate to their surroundings or are of poor stock which takes time to become fully evident – then you are the loser in two ways. First, your hopes are not going to be realised; second, you are going to lose time – and, in gardening terms, a mistake which loses you even two or three years is not to be taken lightly.

And there is something else. It is pointless buying the best plants available if, when you come to get them in the ground, you do not pay full attention to adopting correct planting techniques and, as a natural link with that, find them homes where they will have the best possible chance to thrive. That means the right soil conditions within reasonably narrow limits; the right aspect and degree of sunshine or light shade (if that is important), and, in many instances, protection of some kind from cutting winds. All this adds up to providing what we gardeners call the right microclimate. It's important.

Vast numbers of garden plants are available for us to make use of, and those included here can only be considered a representative selection. They are all very well worth getting to know and my hope would be that trying your hand with some of them will encourage you to cast your net wider still. After a lifetime of gardening I'm as eager as ever to get my hands on new plants – or, if not new in the strict sense, new to me. After all, that is what gardening is all about.

Percy Thrower

Useful Facts

The aim of this book is to provide the gardener with a guide to the appearance and cultivation requirements of a wide range of good garden plants and in this respect the following points may assist the reader to get the best from the book.

Plant types

First a word about the various kinds of plants. In general these are divided into two types: the herbaceous which have soft stems and the woody which have woody stems.

The herbaceous are further subdivided into annuals, biennials and perennials.

Annuals are plants which complete their growth cycle within one year and die after they have flowered and set seed. These are pulled up and discarded after flowering, and must be renewed from seed each year.

Biennials are plants which take two years to complete their life cycles. During the first year they produce foliage only and during the second year they produce flowers, set seed and die. They are also discarded after flowering and must be renewed from seed each year.

Perennials are plants which flower each year and live for a number of years. Many die down to ground level in autumn and grow up again in spring. They can be grown from seed but usually once established they are renewed by division of the root clumps.

Woody plants take a lot longer than the herbaceous plants to reach a state of maturity but having done so they usually live for many years. The main division in this group is into deciduous – those kinds which shed their leaves in autumn and produce fresh ones the following spring – and the evergreens – those which retain their leaves throughout the year.

Both herbaceous and woody plants can be further divided into three categories: the hardy ones which will survive cold winters, the half-hardies or slightly tender which are likely to be killed by frost in cool climates and which, therefore, must be grown in a frost-proof place such as a greenhouse from the late autumn to late spring, and the tender kinds which will only grow outdoors in warm climates and elsewhere must be grown in warm greenhouse or conservatory conditions.

The plants in this book are placed in groups according to their types or their main use, but it should be remembered that many of these groups overlap. For example, trees and shrubs also occur in climbers, hedges and conifers, and some bulbs and herbaceous perennials make good rock plants.

Plant names

Plant names seem to be a major cause of concern to many gardeners. The botanical names are a mixture of Latin, Greek and made-up names with Latinised endings and, awkward as they may appear to pronounce, they are the only accurate way of identifying a particular plant. Common names, many of which are most attractive, vary from place to place and may cause confusion. The plants in this book are listed under their most usual common name and also their botanical names and are placed in alphabetical order of the latter. There is an index to each type of name at the end of the book.

Now a word of explanation about botanical names. The first name is known as the generic name and indicates the genus to which a plant belongs. The second name is a specific name, or if you like a Christian name, and this provides a more exact identification of the plant, often describing a special feature such as the leaves or flower. Further names, if they occur, may be required to complete the identification. Names which appear in quotation marks indicate a selected or hybrid variety which has been developed in cultivation. Names with a 'x' between the generic and specific names such as *Salvia × superba*, also indicate a strain of hybrids which has arisen as a result of several crosses and the exact parentage may be unknown.

To take an example: *Geranium grandiflorum* 'Johnson's Blue'

    Geranium – the genus
    grandiflorum – the specific name, in this case meaning large flowered
    'Johnson's Blue' – a cultivated variety of *Geranium grandiflorum*

Seasons

In gardening it is very difficult to be precise about the time of year when flowering should take place or the various cultivation jobs be carried out – much depends on the temperature and the length of day and this varies a great deal from place to place and country to country.

As a rough guide the seasons mentioned can be defined in terms of months as follows:

For the Northern Hemisphere
Spring   March to May
Summer   June to August
Autumn   September to November
Winter   December to February

For the Southern Hemisphere
Spring   September to November
Summer   December to February
Autumn   March to May
Winter   June to August

Increasing Plants

Cuttings

Soft stem cuttings are prepared when the growth is young and succulent in late spring and early summer. Cut below a leaf joint, trim off any lower leaves and then insert around the edge of a pot in a peat/sand mixture. Water well. Keep in a propagator or place inside a plastic bag and keep shaded

Root cuttings are a means of increase for some of the plants with fairly thick roots. They are usually taken in winter and the thinner, more fibrous cuttings are laid on their sides in seed trays. Thicker cuttings are inserted the right way up in pots of compost. Cut the bottom end on the slant to help differentiate between top and bottom

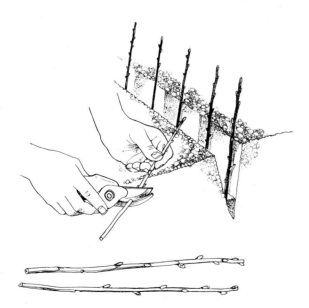

Hardwood cuttings are prepared in autumn from wood which is fully ripe and firm. Cut a piece of shoot about 23 cm (9 in) long, trim the top and end and line out in a shallow trench in a sheltered part of the garden

Half-ripe and heeled cuttings are prepared in summer from shoots which are becoming woody. To make a heeled cutting remove the shoot with a snag of the mature wood from the main stem. This is trimmed and the cutting dipped into hormone rooting powder and then inserted in a pot

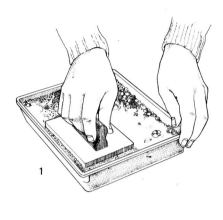

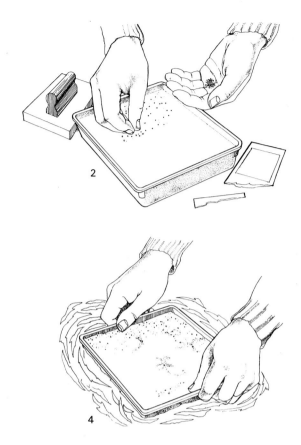

Seed Sowing Indoors

After filling the tray, or pot, with one of the proprietary seed composts the surface is made level and the compost firm with a flat piece of wood (1). The seeds are then sprinkled thinly over the surface (2). More compost is sifted over the seeds until they are just covered (3). The tray is placed in water until this seeps through to the surface (4). The tray is then allowed to drain and covered with a sheet of glass and newspaper until germination has occurred, when both should be removed

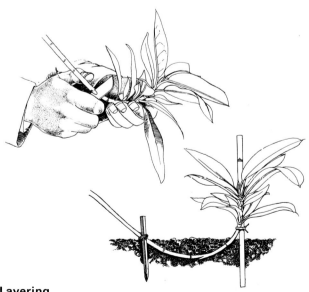

Once the seeds have germinated they should be moved to another tray to give them sufficient space for their subsequent growth. This should be done carefully so that the delicate stems are not damaged. Handle each seedling by the leaves

Layering

A method of increase in which the stem is slit and the shoot is bent down and pegged into the soil where it will make roots. It is best done in spring or early summer

Ornamental Trees and Shrubs

I cannot imagine that anyone is likely to question the importance of trees and shrubs in the modern garden. Even the smallest can find room for something like the weeping flowering cherry, *Prunus* Kiku Shidare Sakura, or the maple *Acer palmatum dissectum*, while small shrubs are available in wide variety. For the larger garden the choice is almost bewildering.

Forming the framework of the garden with trees and shrubs is called foundation planting, a very descriptive phrase. Balance counts for a lot in garden making and when adding trees and shrubs to the garden there is need for especial care in relating one to another, whether in terms of the feature offered (flowers, berries, good foliage or bark effect), or the size and shape and the category (deciduous, evergreen or coniferous).

One thing I cannot stress enough with regard to both trees and shrubs and that is to take note of their ultimate height and spread. It is often very difficult to be really accurate about this for so much depends on the conditions prevailing (soil, climate, amount of light), but one can always make a rough guess at how much space a particular specimen is going to need. Allow them plenty of room, and remember that with slow-maturing trees you can always plant around them with shrubs which can be either moved elsewhere or sacrificed at a later date. Plants which fall in the ground-cover category can be pressed into this kind of service, and you will find many offered in the catalogues of specialist nurseries.

Again, with trees and large shrubs be careful not to plant these in positions where, when mature, they will darken rooms in the house – it is something which is often overlooked. With ground-cover plantings, it is especially important that the soil preparation should be thorough, not only in terms of making sure that the quality and texture is right but also in terms of weed elimination.

Another thing which needs emphasis here: there is no difficulty at all in having colour and interest from trees and shrubs throughout the year. Plan your garden planting to take full advantage of that fact – shrubs like the winter-flowering viburnums, the winter-flowering heathers (varieties of *Erica carnea*), hamamelis (witch hazels) and winter-flowering *Chimonanthus praecox* (winter sweet) can be a joy.

Planting

And now for the practical aspects of tree and shrub cultivation. Trees and shrubs are likely to remain in position for a long time so good soil preparation is all important. Dig it well and work in some organic matter in the form of well-rotted manure or compost and finish with a sprinkling of bonemeal applied at the rate of 85 g per square metre (3 oz per square yard). More and more are being offered as container-grown specimens, which can be planted at any time of year when the weather and soil conditions are suitable. It's a great convenience, and if the plants are treated with due respect at planting time (above all, the root ball must be kept intact) and they are given proper aftercare they will grow on without any check.

But many plants must still be obtained as lifted open-ground nursery stock and for this, of course, there is a very definite planting season, differing somewhat between deciduous and evergreen. Deciduous trees and shrubs lifted from the open ground can be planted between mid-autumn and early spring, whenever the ground is free of frost and is not over-wet.

Evergreens can be planted between early to mid-autumn and in spring. What must always be remembered is that evergreen plants are never in a state of dormancy, so it is vital that re-establishment should be rapid to counteract the loss of moisture which is always taking place through the leaves. Wind, even more than strong sunshine, is a cause of moisture loss and it helps greatly to erect a temporary screen of hessian or plastic material on the side of the prevailing wind during the establishment period.

The planting hole must always be of sufficient size to take the roots at their full spread. Work good soil in among the roots of bare-rooted specimens, and with balled specimens take great care to keep the ball of roots intact, just as you would with a plant removed from a container.

The soil mark on the stem (indicating the depth to which the tree or shrub was planted in the nursery) should be your guide to the correct depth of planting. It is almost always clearly visible.

Newly planted trees must be given firm support, and the stake should be positioned before planting to avoid any possibility of damaging the roots. Make one tie just below the head of branches and another halfway down the stem.

Aftercare

In the spring and summer following planting watch particularly the need for water, for this is a crucial period in their development.

Feed young trees each spring with a dressing of organic matter or with a good compound fertiliser applied at a rate of 85 g per square metre (3 oz per square yard) and even if they are eventually to be grown in grass, keep a cultivated circle of at least 120 cm (4 ft) in diameter around each one for the first few years.

Pruning

Very few ornamental trees require pruning other than the removal of dead or overcrowded branches and suckers coming from the roots. As a general rule, spring-flowering shrubs are pruned after flowering when the wood which has just flowered is cut out, whilst summer-flowering shrubs are pruned in early spring as these flower on wood produced in the current year.

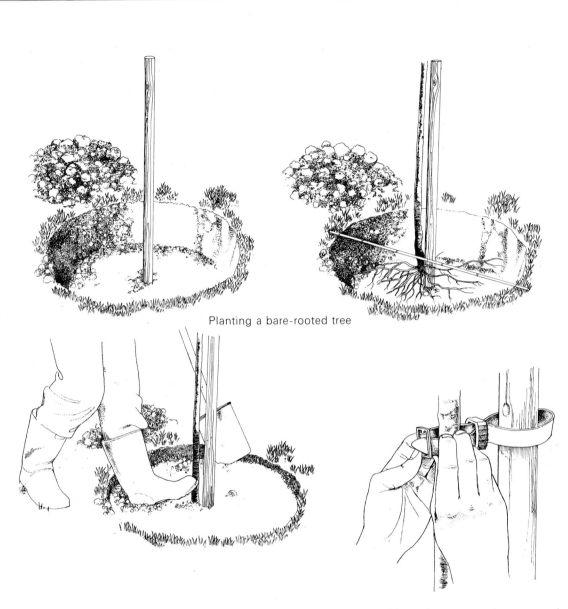

Planting a bare-rooted tree

Use a tie to secure the stem to the
stake

Planting a container-grown shrub

Paperbark Maple
Acer griseum

Site: sun or partial shade

Soil: well drained, moist

Height: up to 4.5 m (15 ft)

Spread: up to 2.5 m (8 ft)

Type of tree: hardy, deciduous

Flowers: insignificant

Fruits: bunches of downy 'keys', each one with two wings at an angle

Planting time: mid to late autumn or early to mid spring

Propagation: sow seeds as soon as ripe or stratify first and then sow

Pruning: none required

Uses: good specimen tree with attractive bark; the old bark peels to reveal new red-orange bark underneath. Marvellous autumn colouring

Japanese Maple
Acer palmatum 'Dissectum'

Site: sun or partial shade with shelter from strong winds

Soil: well drained, moist

Height: slow growing, up to 4.5 m (15 ft)

Spread: up to 2.5 m (8 ft)

Type of tree: hardy, deciduous

Flowers: insignificant

Flowering time: early summer

Fruits: bunches of two-winged fruits or 'keys'

Planting time: mid to late autumn or early to mid spring

Propagation: graft onto an *Acer palmatum* rootstock

Pruning: none required

Uses: very decorative shrub or small tree with spectacular autumn colour; purple-leaved variety 'Atropurpureum' available

Snowy Mespilus

Amelanchier lamarckii

Site: partial shade or sun

Soil: well drained but moist, free of lime

Height: up to 6 m (20 ft)

Spread: up to 3 m (10 ft)

Type of tree: hardy, deciduous

Flowers: small white flowers carried in profusion

Flowering time: mid to late spring

Planting time: early to mid spring or mid to late autumn

Propagation: sow seeds in summer or stratify and then sow; layer branches in early autumn; separate and plant rooted suckers from mid autumn to early spring

Pruning: none required

Uses: decorative spring-flowering tree with spectacular autumn colour

Bog Rosemary

Andromeda polifolia

Site: partial shade or sun

Soil: moist, peaty, lime-free

Height: 30 cm (1 ft)

Spread: 30 cm (1 ft)

Type of shrub: hardy, evergreen

Flowers: clusters of pink blooms

Flowering time: late spring to early summer

Planting time: early spring or late summer or early autumn

Propagation: sow seeds in spring in peaty soil or layer shoots in spring

Pruning: remove any dead wood

Uses: this dwarf shrub is especially suitable for damp rock gardens or peat beds. There are a number of good varieties including 'Compacta' and the nearly prostrate 'Minima'

Japanese Angelica Tree
Aralia elata

Site: partial shade or sun, sheltered

Soil: rich and fertile, moist but well drained

Height: up to 10 m (33 ft)

Spread: up to 5 m (16 ft)

Type of tree: hardy, deciduous

Flowers: small, white, borne in clusters up to 45 cm (18 in) long

Flowering time: late summer and early autumn

Planting time: mid to late autumn or early to mid spring

Propagation: stratify seeds and sow in 15 to 18°C (59 to 64°F); dig up rooted suckers in autumn

Pruning: remove dead or frost-damaged wood in spring

Uses: as a specimen tree grown mainly for its huge decorative leaves; variegated forms available 'Aureovariegata' and 'Variegata'

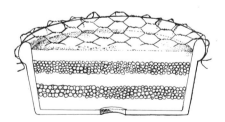

Germination can be improved by stratification. The seeds are placed between layers of sand and kept cool throughout the winter before being sown in spring.

Spotted Laurel
Aucuba japonica 'Variegata'

Site: partial shade or sun

Soil: ordinary

Height: up to 3.5 m (11 ft)

Spread: up to 2 m (6 ft)

Type of shrub: hardy, evergreen

Flowers: olive green, star shaped

Flowering time: early to mid spring

Fruits: bright red berries produced on female plants appear in autumn through to the following spring if a male plant is nearby to ensure pollination

Planting time: early to mid spring or late summer to early autumn. Male and female forms must both be planted if berries are required

Propagation: sow seeds in autumn; heeled cuttings 10 cm (4 in) long can be taken in late summer or early autumn and inserted into a peat/sand compost in a cold frame

Pruning: none required

Uses: small plants can be planted in containers or window-boxes; they are tolerant of atmospheric pollution and fairly dense shade

Barberry

Berberis darwinii

Site: partial shade or sun

Soil: well drained garden soil, tolerates thin and limy soils

Height: up to 2.5 m (8 ft)

Spread: up to 2.5 m (8 ft)

Type of shrub: hardy evergreen, also deciduous kinds

Flowers: yellow or orange, carried in clusters

Flowering time: mid to late spring

Fruits: blue-black berries follow the flowers

Planting time: early spring or mid to late autumn

Propagation: sow seeds in late autumn; heeled cuttings 10 cm (4 in) long can be taken in late summer or early autumn and inserted in a peat/sand compost in a cold frame

Pruning: cut out old stems and trim straggly growth after flowering

Uses: suitable for use as a hedge. This is one species of a large group of beautiful deciduous and evergreen shrubs. The deciduous kinds have good autumn colouring. See also page 76

Fruits of *Berberis darwinii*

Young's Weeping Birch

Betula pendula 'Youngii'

Site: partial shade or sun

Soil: well drained, will tolerate thin or sandy soil

Height: up to 6 m (20 ft)

Spread: up to 2.5 m (8 ft)

Type of tree: hardy, deciduous

Flowers: male catkins are pale yellow, female catkins are green and insignificant

Flowering time: early to mid spring

Planting time: early to mid spring or mid to late autumn

Propagation: graft onto *Betula pendula* rootstock; *Betula pendula* itself can be grown from seed sown in early spring

Pruning: none required

Uses: silver bark and weeping form are attractive features of this graceful tree and make it a good choice as a specimen for the small garden

Butterfly Bush

Buddleia davidii

Site: sunny

Soil: well drained, will tolerate dry or limy soil

Height: up to 2.5 m (8 ft)

Spread: up to 2.5 m (8 ft)

Type of shrub: hardy, deciduous

Flowers: clusters of white, cream, red, purple or violet blooms according to variety

Flowering time: mid to late summer

Planting time: early spring or mid to late autumn

Propagation: take 10 cm (4 in) heeled cuttings of lateral shoots in mid to late summer and insert in a peat/sand compost in a cold frame; alternatively take 30 cm (1 ft) hardwood cuttings in mid autumn and set in open soil outdoors

Pruning: cut hard back to within 5 cm (2 in) of old wood in early spring

Uses: attracts butterflies; a number of named varieties are available, look for 'Black Knight' deep violet, 'Pink Pearl' lilac pink, 'Royal Red' reddish purple, and 'White Cloud'

Box

Buxus sempervirens

Site: partial shade or sun

Soil: alkaline or ordinary

Height: slow growing, up to 3 m (10 ft)

Spread: up to 1.5 m (5 ft)

Type of shrub: hardy, evergreen

Flowers: inconspicuous, pale green

Flowering time: mid to late spring

Planting time: early to mid spring or early to mid autumn

Propagation: take 10 cm (4 in) long cuttings in late summer or early autumn and insert in a peat/sand compost in a cold frame

Pruning: clip hedges in late summer or early autumn

Uses: can be used as a dwarf hedging plant and is suitable for topiary work. See also page 76

Ling, Heather

Calluna vulgaris

Site: partial shade or sun

Soil: dry to moist, lime-free

Height: up to 60 cm (2 ft)

Spread: up to 60 cm (2 ft)

Type of shrub: hardy, evergreen

Flowers: white, cream, purple or violet according to variety

Flowering time: early summer to mid autumn

Planting time: early to mid spring or mid to late autumn

Propagation: by division in spring or autumn; take cuttings of side shoots about 5 cm (2 in) long from midsummer to mid autumn and insert into a sandy compost

Pruning: remove dead flowers, do not cut back into older wood

Uses: good ground cover plants

Blue Spiraea

Caryopteris × clandonensis

Site: warm, sunny, sheltered

Soil: well drained, tolerates alkaline conditions

Height: up to 1 m (3 ft)

Spread: up to 1 m (3 ft)

Type of shrub: hardy, deciduous

Flowers: blue, carried in clusters

Flowering time: late to early autumn

Planting time: early to mid spring or early to mid autumn

Propagation: take 10 cm (4 in) cuttings in late summer and insert in peat/sand compost in a cold frame

Pruning: cut back previous year's growth to two buds in early spring; remove any weak growth

Uses: charming small shrubs with aromatic grey foliage, ideal for a mixed border. The hybrids are hardier: 'Arthur Simmonds' bright blue, 'Ferndown' blue-violet

Indian Bean Tree
Catalpa bignonioides

Site: partial shade or sun

Soil: good, well drained

Height: up to 9 m (30 ft)

Spread: up to 6 m (20 ft)

Type of tree: hardy, deciduous

Flowers: erect clusters of white flowers marked with purple and yellow

Flowering time: midsummer

Fruits: long slender green pods

Planting time: mid autumn to early spring

Propagation: take 10 cm (4 in) heeled cuttings in midsummer, insert in sandy compost in a temperature of 13 to 18°C (55 to 64°F)

Pruning: none required; branches can be cut back in winter if trees are overgrown

Uses: ornamental tree which comes into leaf very late; there is a golden-leaved form 'Aurea'

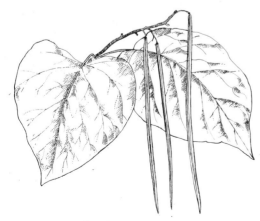

Seedpods of catalpa

Californian Lilac, Ceanothus
Ceanothus

Site: sun

Soil: light, well drained

Height: up to 4.5 m (15 ft)

Spread: up to 3 m (10 ft)

Type of shrub: deciduous or slightly tender evergreen according to species

Flowers: blue, violet, pink

Flowering time: early spring to mid autumn according to variety or species

Planting time: mid to late spring or early autumn, container-grown plants are easier to establish

Propagation: take 10 cm (4 in) heeled cuttings in midsummer, insert in a peat/sand compost in a temperature of 15°C (59°F)

Pruning: prune deciduous varieties hard back to within 8 cm (3 in) of the old wood in mid spring; evergreen species do not need pruning except for trimming off previous year's shoots to keep a good shape

Uses: can be trained as very decorative wall shrubs. The evergreen species such as *C. impressus*, deep blue, *C. rigidus*, purplish-blue, and *C. thyrsiflorus* flower in late spring and early summer, whilst the deciduous kinds flower in late summer – look for 'Gloire de Versailles' blue, 'Perle Rose' pink

Leadwort, Hardy Plumbago

Ceratostigma

Site: sun

Soil: light, well drained

Height: up to 1 m (3 ft)

Spread: up to 1 m (3 ft)

Type of shrub: hardy or slightly tender, deciduous shrubs or herbaceous perennials

Flowers: blue

Flowering time: late summer to early autumn according to variety

Planting time: early to late spring

Propagation: take 8 cm (3 in) heeled cuttings in midsummer, insert into peat/sand compost with bottom heat

Pruning: cut out old or dying shoots in early spring

Uses: useful late-flowering shrub; attractive autumn colour. *C. plumbaginoides* is herbaceous, 15 to 30 cm (6 to 12 in) tall and useful in rock gardens. *C. willmottianum* is more shrubby, 90 cm (3 ft) high and good for shrub or mixed borders; it may be killed to ground level by frost but will usually spring up again

Flowering Quince, Japonica,

Chaenomeles

Site: sun or semi-shade

Soil: ordinary

Height: up to 2 m (6 ft)

Spread: up to 2.25 m (7 ft)

Type of shrub: hardy, deciduous

Flowers: white, orange, pink and red according to variety

Flowering time: late winter to mid spring

Fruits: yellow fruits which can be used to make quince jelly

Planting time: late winter to early spring or mid to late autumn

Propagation: layering branches in early autumn; take 10 cm (4 in) heeled cuttings in mid to late summer and insert into a peat/sand compost with bottom heat; sow seeds in early autumn

Pruning: hedges should be trimmed after flowering; when grown as a bush, thin out crowded branches; when trained against a wall all shoots that cannot be tied in should be shortened to five leaves in summer

Uses: can be trained against walls if tied in to wires or trellis; can be grown as an informal hedge. There are many good varieties including 'Knap Hill Scarlet', 'Moerloosii', pale pink and 'Nivalis' white

Winter Sweet

Chimonanthus praecox

Site: sunny, sheltered – blossoms easily damaged by frost

Soil: deep, rich, well drained

Height: up to 3 m (10 ft)

Spread: up to 2.5 m (8 ft)

Type of shrub: hardy, deciduous

Flowers: yellow, very fragrant

Flowering time: mid winter to early spring

Planting time: late winter to early spring or mid to late autumn

Propagation: sow seeds in early autumn; layer shoots in early or mid autumn or spring

Pruning: prune after flowering, cutting out some of the older branches

Uses: can be trained as a wall shrub for those aspects which receive some sun and are sheltered from strong winds

Clethra

Clethra barbinervis

Site: sun or light shade

Soil: rich, moist, lime-free

Height: up to 9 m (30 ft)

Spread: up to 6 m (20 ft)

Type of shrub: hardy, deciduous

Flowers: white

Flowering time: midsummer to early autumn

Planting time: early to mid spring or mid to late autumn

Propagation: bud or graft onto a *Crataegus monogyna* in mid autumn; take 10 cm (4 in) heeled cuttings of side shoots and insert in a peat/sand compost with bottom heat in midsummer

Pruning: none required, some of the older stems may be cut out each winter if wished

Uses: the scented flowers and autumn colouring of the leaves make it a pleasant specimen tree

Bladder Senna

Colutea × *media*

Site: sun or partial shade

Soil: ordinary

Height: up to 3 m (10 ft)

Spread: up to 3 m (10 ft)

Type of shrub: hardy, deciduous

Flowers: brownish-red, pea-like

Flowering time: late spring to late summer

Fruits: green inflated pods which give the shrub its common name

Planting time: late winter to early spring or mid to late autumn

Propagation: sow seeds in early spring; take 10 cm (4 in) heeled cuttings of side shoots and insert in a peat/sand compost in summer or early autumn

Uses: suitable for hot dry places

Red-Barked Dogwood

Cornus alba 'Elegantissima'

Site: partial shade or sun

Soil: moist

Height: up to 3 m (10 ft)

Spread: up to 3 m (10 ft)

Type of shrub: hardy, deciduous

Flowers: white, insignificant

Flowering time: late spring and early summer

Fruits: white berries

Planting time: early to mid spring

Propagation: sow seeds in late summer or early autumn; layer shoots in spring; take 10 cm (4 in) heeled cuttings and insert in a peat/sand compost in summer or autumn; detach rooted suckers in autumn and replant at once

Pruning: cut hard back to within a few inches of the ground in mid spring to encourage the production of the brilliant red stems

Uses: bright red stems bring colour in winter; attractive variegated foliage in summer

Dogwood

Cornus kousa

Site: partial shade or sun

Soil: ordinary

Height: up to 3 m (10 ft)

Spread: up to 3 m (10 ft)

Type of shrub: hardy, deciduous

Flowers: purple-green flowers surrounded by white bracts

Flowering time: late spring to early summer

Fruits: red, strawberry-like in late summer

Planting time: early to late autumn

Propagation: sow seeds in late summer or early autumn; layer shoots in spring; take 10 cm (4 in) heeled cuttings and insert in a peat/sand compost in summer or autumn

Pruning: none required

Uses: the showy bracts which surround the insignificant flowers make a fine display in spring

Corylopsis

Corylopsis

Site: sun or partial shade

Soil: deep, fairly rich, preferably slightly acid

Height: up to 3 m (10 ft)

Spread: up to 3 m (10 ft)

Type of shrub: hardy, deciduous

Flowers: yellow

Flowering time: early to mid spring

Planting time: late to early spring or mid to late autumn

Propagation: layer shoots in mid autumn; take 10 cm (4 in) heeled cuttings and insert in a peat/sand compost with bottom heat in mid or late summer

Pruning: none required

Uses: the fragrant spring flowers are a feature of this shrub but they may be damaged by frost so it is better to plant it in a sheltered position

Corkscrew Hazel

Corylus avellana 'Contorta'

Site: best in sun but will tolerate very light shade

Soil: well drained, rich

Height: up to 3 m (10 ft)

Spread: up to 3 m (10 ft)

Type of tree: hardy, deciduous

Flowers: yellow male catkins, small crimson female flowers

Flowering time: early to mid spring

Fruits: edible brown cobnuts

Planting time: late winter to early spring or mid to late autumn

Propagation: layer shoots in autumn; sow seeds (nuts) in mid to late autumn in the garden

Pruning: little required, cut out damaged or ingrowing stems and suckers in winter

Uses: the coiled and twisted branches make this an unusual specimen tree

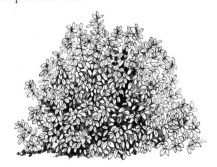

Smoke Tree

Cotinus coggygria

Site: sunny

Soil: well drained, ordinary

Height: up to 2.5 m (8 ft)

Spread: up to 2.5 m (8 ft)

Type of shrub: hardy, deciduous

Flowers: pale purple, feathery

Flowering time: early to midsummer

Planting time: late winter to early spring or mid to late autumn

Propagation: layer shoots in early autumn; take 13 cm (5 in) heeled cuttings and insert in a peat/sand compost in late summer; dig up rooted suckers in autumn

Pruning: none required but if overgrown the previous year's stems can be shortened to two buds in early spring

Uses: the feathery inflorescences and rich purple autumn colour of the foliage are assets of this plant which make it a good choice for a mixed border or for use as a specimen

Cotoneaster

Cotoneaster salicifolia

Site: sun or partial shade

Soil: ordinary

Height: up to 3.75 m (12 ft)

Spread: up to 3.75 m (12 ft)

Type of shrub: hardy, evergreen

Flowers: white

Flowering time: early summer

Fruits: red berries following the flowers and often persisting into winter

Planting time: late winter to early spring or mid to late autumn

Propagation: sow seeds in spring; take 10 cm (4 in) heeled cuttings in mid to late summer and insert in a peat/sand compost; take hardwood cuttings in autumn and root outdoors

Pruning: none required

Uses: useful for screening. This is one species of a very useful large group of evergreen and deciduous flowering and berry-bearing shrubs. All require the same conditions and some make good wall plants, see page 58

Hawthorn, May

Crataegus oxyacantha 'Paul's Scarlet'

Site: semi-shade or sun

Soil: ordinary

Height: up to 6 m (20 ft)

Spread: up to 4.5 m (15 ft)

Type of tree: hardy, deciduous

Flowers: scarlet, double

Flowering time: late spring and early summer

Planting time: late winter to early spring or mid to late autumn

Propagation: bud or graft onto a *Crataegus monogyna* rootstock in spring: *C. oxyacantha* itself can be grown from seed

Pruning: none required but if overgrown branches may be cut back in winter

Uses: makes a good hedge or screen; tolerant of exposure and atmospheric pollution. There are many other good varieties such as 'Plena' double white flowers, 'Rosea' single pink flowers and 'Rosea Flore Plena' double pink. See also p. 78

Warminster Broom

Cytisus × praecox

Site: sunny

Soil: rather poor, well drained, tolerant of lime

Height: up to 2 m (6 ft)

Spread: up to 2 m (6 ft)

Type of shrub: hardy, deciduous

Flowers: cream or pale yellow, pea-like

Flowering time: mid to late spring

Planting time: early to mid spring or early to mid autumn

Propagation: take heeled cuttings 8 to 10 cm (3 to 4 in) long and insert in peat and sand in a frame in late summer

Pruning: little required, when necessary cut back shoots by about two-thirds when flowering is over – do not cut back into old hard wood

Uses: a small delightful shrub for the rock garden or any position where it can display its thin arching stems of blooms. There are several other brooms, varying in height and flower colour; all require the same conditions but may not be long lived. In general, they resent disturbance of the roots. *C. battandieri*, the Moroccan broom, is especially attractive with its large clusters of yellow pineapple-scented flowers in summer good for training against a sunny wall

St Dabeoc's Heath

Daboecia cantabrica

Site: sunny

Soil: lime-free, sandy peat

Height: up to 60 cm (2 ft)

Spread: up to 60 cm (2 ft)

Type of shrub: hardy, evergreen

Flowers: white, cream, pink, red or purple according to variety

Flowering time: early summer to early autumn

Planting time: early to mid spring or mid to late autumn

Propagation: layer shoots in autumn; take 5-cm (2-in) cuttings from young side shoots in midsummer to early autumn and insert in a sandy compost in a cold frame or propagator

Pruning: clip off dead flower stems in the spring

Uses: can be used for ground cover; several named varieties available

Daphne

Daphne × burkwoodii

Site: sun or semi-shade

Soil: ordinary, well drained

Height: up to 1 m (3 ft)

Spread: up to 1 m (3 ft)

Type of shrub: hardy, semi-evergreen

Flowers: pink, sweetly scented

Flowering time: late spring to early summer

Planting time: early to mid spring or early to mid autumn

Propagation: take 8 cm (3 in) cuttings from young side shoots and insert into a peat/sand compost in a cold frame

Pruning: none required

Uses: pretty shrub for the rock garden or front of a border. There are other good evergreen species such as *D. odora*, 60 to 90 cm (2 to 3 ft), white, early spring flowers; *D. collina*, 30 to 45 cm (12 to 18 in), purple flowers in late spring. Deciduous species include *D. mezereum*, 90 cm (3 ft), purple flowers in late winter and *D. genkwa*, 60 to 90 cm (2 to 3 ft), lavender-blue spring flowers. All require the same conditions

Deutzia

Deutzia × hybrida 'Magician'

Site: sun or partial shade

Soil: ordinary, well drained

Height: up to 2 m (6 ft)

Spread: up to 1.5 m (5 ft)

Type of shrub: hardy, deciduous

Flowers: pink edged with white

Flowering time: early to midsummer

Planting time: mid to late autumn or late winter to early spring

Propagation: take 10 cm (4 in) cuttings of young shoots in mid to late summer and insert in a peat/sand compost

Pruning: cut out flowered shoots when flowering is over

Uses: a handsome plant for the border, noted for the elegant sprays of flowers. Other good varieties are 'Pride of Rochester' double white flowers flushed with purple, 'Boule de Neige' single, white, 'Mont Rose', single, rose pink. There are also many species but all require the same conditions

Elaeagnus

Elaeagnus pungens 'Maculata'

Site: sun or semi-shade

Soil: ordinary, well drained; will tolerate limy soils

Height: up to 3 m (10 ft)

Spread: up to 3 m (10 ft)

Type of shrub: hardy, evergreen

Flowers: small, silvery white, fragrant

Flowering time: mid to late autumn

Planting time: mid spring or early autumn

Propagation: take 10 cm (4 in) cuttings in late summer or early autumn and insert in a peat/sand compost in a cold frame

Pruning: none required but cut out any shoots where the leaves have reverted to an all-green colour

Uses: the bright variegated foliage makes this a valuable shrub in winter. Fast growing and tolerant of exposure to winds (even salt ones); will grow almost anywhere and makes a good hedge or wind screen

Enkianthus

Enkianthus campanulatus

Site: sun or semi-shade, sheltered

Soil: ordinary, lime-free, added peat or leafmould an advantage

Height: up to 2.5 m (8 ft)

Spread: up to 1.25 m (4 ft)

Type of shrub: hardy, deciduous

Flowers: cream veined with red, bell shaped

Flowering time: late spring

Planting time: early spring or mid to late autumn

Propagation: sow seeds in peaty soil in spring; take 8 cm (3 in) heeled cuttings in early to mid autumn

Pruning: none required

Uses: good autumn colour and pretty flowers make this an interesting border plant. Useful in thin woodland

Heather

Erica carnea 'Springwood White'

Site: best in sun, will tolerate light shade

Soil: sandy-peat soil, will tolerate lime

Height: up to 30 cm (1 ft)

Spread: up to 60 cm (2 ft)

Type of shrub: hardy evergreen

Flowers: sprigs of white bells

Flowering time: late autumn to late spring

Planting time: early to late spring or mid to late autumn

Propagation: take 2.5 cm (1 in) cuttings of young side shoots and insert in a sandy compost in a mist propagator if possible; layer shoots in spring

Pruning: clip over plant with shears after flowering

Uses: good ground cover plant; *E. carnea* has many named varieties which range in colour from white to deep pink. There are many other heathers, some of which have delightful foliage colours, but the majority will not grow on soils containing lime

Escallonia

Escallonia 'Donard Seedling'

Site: sunny

Soil: ordinary, well drained

Height: up to 2 m (6 ft)

Spread: up to 1.5 m (5 ft)

Type of shrub: hardy evergreen

Flowers: pale pink

Flowering time: early to midsummer

Planting time: early spring or mid autumn

Propagation: take 10 cm (4 in) heeled cuttings in late summer or early autumn and insert in sand; layer shoots in spring

Pruning: remove old flowering growths immediately after flowering

Uses: especially good in seaside locations as some kinds are not completely hardy in cool climates. They make good hedges and windbreaks. There are many other species and named varieties with flowers ranging from white to red in colour; notable are 'Apple Blossom' pale pink, 'C. F. Ball' red, 'Glasnevin Hybrid' red, 'Langleyensis' rose-pink

Euonymus

Euonymus fortunei

Site: sun or shade (this plant tolerates quite deep shade); needs a sheltered spot

Soil: ordinary

Height: will grow to 3 m (10 ft) against a wall

Spread: up to 1.5 m (5 ft)

Type of shrub: hardy, trailing, evergreen

Flowers: insignificant green-white

Flowering time: late spring to early summer

Fruits: pink capsules containing orange seeds

Planting time: mid to late spring or early to mid autumn

Propagation: take 10 cm (4 in) heeled cuttings in late summer or early autumn and insert them into a peat/sand compost

Pruning: trim if necessary in midsummer; cut hard back in spring if desired

Uses: attractive ground cover or climbing plant, especially in its variegated forms such as 'Silver Queen'

Pearl Bush

Exochorda racemosa

Site: sunny, not too dry

Soil: ordinary, rather moist

Height: 3 m (10 ft)

Spread: 2.5 m (8 ft)

Type of shrub: hardy, deciduous

Flowers: white

Flowering time: late spring

Planting time: early spring or early to mid autumn

Propagation: sow seeds in spring or autumn; take 10 cm (4 in) cuttings of young shoots in early to midsummer and insert in a sand/peat compost

Pruning: shorten shoots that have flowered back to young growths, doing this immediately after flowering

Uses: this beautiful flowering shrub should be used more often as a specimen plant. There are other species but all require the same conditions

Forsythia

Forsythia × intermedia

Site: sun or light shade

Soil: ordinary

Height: up to 3 m (10 ft)

Spread: up to 2.25 m (7 ft)

Type of shrub: hardy, deciduous

Flowers: yellow

Flowering time: early to mid spring

Planting time: early spring or mid to late autumn

Propagation: take 25 cm (10 in) hardwood cuttings in mid autumn and root outdoors; especially easy by layering shoots in autumn, this often happens naturally

Pruning: trim shrub over to keep a good shape in mid spring after flowering, cutting back the old flowering stems to new shoots. Do not cut out any stems which have not flowered.

Uses: one of the most welcome of the spring-flowering shrubs, it also makes a good informal hedge and a fast-growing shrub for training against walls. There are a number of varieties and other species, all require the same treatment

Fothergilla

Fothergilla major

Site: sunny, open

Soil: lime-free, fertile

Height: up to 2.5 m (8 ft)

Spread: up to 1.5 m (5 ft)

Type of shrub: hardy, deciduous

Flowers: white, feathery

Flowering time: late spring

Planting time: early spring or mid to late autumn

Propagation: layer shoots in autumn; take cuttings of young shoots in summer and insert in a propagator

Pruning: none required

Uses: the sweetly-scented flowers and brilliant autumn colour of the foliage make this an ideal specimen tree

Golden Ash

Fraxinus excelsior 'Aurea'

Site: sun or semi-shade

Soil: ordinary

Height: up to 15 m (50 ft)

Spread: up to 7.5 m (25 ft)

Type of tree: hardy, deciduous

Flowers: insignificant, yellow-green

Flowering time: mid to late spring

Fruits: clusters of winged fruits known as 'keys'

Planting time: early spring or mid to late autumn

Propagation: graft onto a *Fraxinus excelsior* rootstock in early spring; *Fraxinus excelsior* itself can be raised from seeds stratified and then sown outdoors

Pruning: none required

Uses: golden-yellow autumn colour; specimen tree only suitable for large gardens

Ash 'keys'

Fuchsia

Fuchsia magellanica

Site: sun or light shade, sheltered, a number of species and varieties are tender in cool climates and must be grown in a cool greenhouse or conservatory

Soil: rich, well drained

Height: up to 1.5 m (5 ft)

Spread: up to 1 m (3 ft)

Type of shrub: hardy or half-hardy, deciduous

Flowers: crimson and purple

Flowering time: midsummer to mid autumn

Planting time: mid spring

Propagation: take 10 cm (4 in) tip cuttings from mid spring to early autumn and insert them into sandy compost in a propagator; species can be raised from seeds sown in spring

Pruning: cut down to ground level in early spring or late autumn; trim over greenhouse-grown varieties in late winter

Uses: can be grown as a hedge; there is a large number of species and varieties of varying colour combinations, many are suitable for hanging baskets or growing as standards

Spanish Gorse
Genista hispanica

Site: sunny, open

Soil: light, well drained

Height: up to 1.25 m (4 ft)

Spread: up to 2 m (6 ft)

Type of shrub: hardy, deciduous

Flowers: yellow, pea-like

Flowering time: early to midsummer

Planting time: early spring or mid to late autumn

Propagation: sow seeds in early spring

Pruning: prune after flowering by trimming back the flowering shoots; do not cut into old wood

Uses: thrives on dry banks and in poor, stony ground. Resents root disturbance, plant container-grown specimens if possible. There are a number of other species, the tallest of which, *G. aetnensis*, may grow to 6 m (20 ft). All require the same conditions

Witch Hazel
Hamamelis mollis

Site: sun or partial shade

Soil: slightly acid or neutral, deep and rich

Height: up to 2.5 m (8 ft)

Spread: up to 2.5 m (8 ft)

Type of tree: hardy, deciduous

Flowers: yellow, narrow twisted petals

Flowering time: midwinter

Planting time: early spring or mid to late autumn

Propagation: sow seeds in mid autumn; layer shoots in autumn

Pruning: little required, trim back straggly growth after flowering

Uses: valuable for the sweetly scented winter flowers, also good autumn colouring. Makes a big bush so allow plenty of space. Good in town conditions. There are other species which require the same conditions

Hibiscus

Hibiscus syriacus

Site: sunny and sheltered

Soil: rich, light, fertile, well drained

Height: 2.5 m (8 ft)

Spread: 1.5 m (5 ft)

Type of shrub: hardy, deciduous

Flowers: white, pink, crimson, purple or violet according to variety

Flowering time: early to mid autumn

Planting time: early spring or early to mid autumn

Propagation: take 10 cm (4 in) heeled cuttings in early to midsummer and insert in a peat/sand compost

Pruning: no regular pruning required, cut out thin and dead wood in spring

Uses: good, late-flowering shrub. There are many varieties, such of which have double flowers

Sea Buckthorn

Hippophae rhamnoides

Site: sunny, open or light shade

Soil: well drained, sandy or ordinary

Height: up to 3 m (10 ft)

Spread: up to 2.5 m (8 ft)

Type of shrub: hardy, deciduous

Flowers: yellow, inconspicuous, male and female flowers are borne on separate plants

Flowering time: mid spring

Fruits: orange berries are produced on female plants if a male plant is planted nearby for pollination

Planting time: early spring or mid to late autumn

Propagation: sow seeds in mid autumn; layer shoots in autumn

Pruning: cut back straggly growth during late summer

Uses: can be used as an informal hedge or windbreak; thrives in seaside areas

Hydrangea

Hydrangea macrophylla

Site: light shade or sunny, sheltered

Soil: moist, enriched with well-rotted compost or manure; acid soil for blue flowers, alkaline soil for red and pink flowers

Height: up to 3 m (10 ft)

Spread: up to 2 m (6 ft)

Type of shrub: hardy, deciduous

Flowers: red, purple, blue, pink, cream

Flowering time: midsummer to early autumn

Planting time: mid autumn to late autumn or early to mid spring

Propagation: take 10 cm (4 in) long cuttings from non-flowering shoots in late summer or early autumn and insert in a peat/sand compost in a propagator, preferably with bottom heat; layer shoots in autumn

Pruning: remove dead flowering heads and any weak or dead wood in early spring

Uses: dried heads can be used in flower arrangements; plants can be grown in containers for use in cool greenhouses or outdoors on a sheltered terrace or patio

Rose of Sharon

Hypericum calycinum

Site: sun or shade

Soil: ordinary, well drained

Height: up to 30 cm (1 ft)

Spread: up to 2 m (6 ft)

Type of shrub: hardy, evergreen

Flowers: yellow

Flowering time: early summer to early autumn

Planting time: early to mid spring

Propagation: increase by division of roots during autumn or spring; take 5 cm (2 in) cuttings from the base of the plant in late spring or early summer and insert them into a peat/sand compost; sow seeds in spring

Pruning: cut back to the base every few years in spring to encourage dense bushy growth

Uses: excellent ground cover plant especially for banks and under trees

St John's Wort

Hypericum elatum 'Elstead'

Site: sunny

Soil: ordinary, well drained

Height: up to 1.25 m (4 ft)

Spread: up to 1.25 m (4 ft)

Type of shrub: fairly hardy, semi-evergreen

Flowers: yellow

Flowering time: midsummer to early autumn

Fruits: clusters of red berries in autumn

Planting time: early to mid spring

Propagation: take 10 cm (4 in) cuttings with a heel from midsummer to early autumn and insert in sandy soil in a frame

Pruning: cut back hard in early spring to encourage the production of flowering shoots

Uses: useful for flower arrangements; very decorative spreading shrub, best in milder areas

Holly

Ilex

Site: shade or sunny

Soil: ordinary

Height: up to 7.5 m (25 ft)

Spread: up to 4.5 m (15 ft)

Type of shrub: deciduous or evergreen according to variety

Flowers: green male and female flowers often borne on separate trees

Flowering time: mid to late spring

Fruits: red or yellow berries according to variety are freely borne on female trees if male trees are nearby to pollinate them

Planting time: mid to late spring or early to mid autumn

Propagation: species can be grown from seed; graft or bud variegated forms onto common species in spring or summer; take cuttings of half-ripened side shoots with a heel in summer and insert in a peat/sand compost

Pruning: clip over in late spring or early summer

Uses: good for hedges (see page 79) and windbreaks; forms with variegated foliage are available and make fine specimen trees. Once planted they resent root disturbance

Calico Bush

Kalmia latifolia

Site: partial shade, cool, or in sun

Soil: moist, lime-free, good drainage

Height: up to 3 m (10 ft)

Spread: up to 2.5 m (7 ft)

Type of shrub: hardy, evergreen

Flowers: rose-pink in clusters

Flowering time: early summer

Planting time: mid to late spring or early to mid autumn

Propagation: sow seeds in spring in a frame; layer shoots in spring; take 10 cm (4 in) cuttings in late summer or early autumn and insert in a peat/sand compost

Pruning: if necessary shorten straggly growth after flowering

Uses: this charming shrub is good for growing in thin woodland; note that foliage is poisonous to cattle

Jew's Mallow

Kerria japonica pleniflora

Site: sun or light shade

Soil: ordinary

Height: up to 2 m (6 ft)

Spread: up to 1.5 m (5 ft)

Type of shrub: hardy, deciduous

Flowers: yellow

Flowering time: mid to late spring

Planting time: early spring to mid to late autumn

Propagation: layer shoots in spring; remove and replant rooted suckers in mid to late autumn or late winter; take 8 cm (3 in) cuttings in late summer to early autumn and insert in a peat/sand compost

Pruning: cut out old flowering stems down to young growths when flowering is over

Uses: can be trained against a wall or fence

Beauty Bush

Kolkwitzia amabilis

Site: full sun

Soil: well drained

Height: up to 3 m (10 ft)

Spread: up to 2.5 m (8 ft)

Type of shrub: hardy, deciduous

Flowers: pink with a yellow throat

Flowering time: late spring to early summer

Planting time: early spring to mid to late autumn

Propagation: layer in spring or autumn; take 10 cm (4 in) cuttings of non-flowering shoots in mid to late summer and insert in a peat/sand compost

Pruning: cut out old, weak stems after flowering

Uses: the attractive, peeling bark is a feature in winter; makes an attractive shrub for the border. There is a good variety 'Pink Cloud'

Laburnum

Laburnum

Site: flowers best in a sunny open place but will grow in shade

Soil: ordinary

Height: 3 to 5 m (10 to 16 ft)

Spread: 3 to 4 m (10 to 14 ft)

Type of tree: hardy, deciduous

Flowers: yellow

Flowering time: mid spring to early summer

Fruits: slender green pods

Planting time: early spring or mid to late autumn

Propagation: sow seeds in mid autumn; layer in autumn; take cuttings of young growth and insert in a propagator in summer

Pruning: none required; if too big, branches may be shortened in winter

Uses: delightful specimen tree but remember that all parts of this plant are poisonous and it is not a good choice for gardens where children play; the Scotch laburnum, *L. alpinum*, is scented. 'Vossii' is an especially good form

Lavender

Lavendula

Site: warm, sunny

Soil: well drained, good on limy soils

Height: up to 1 m (3 ft)

Spread: up to 1 m (3 ft)

Type of shrub: hardy or slightly tender evergreen

Flowers: spikes of blue-purple or white

Flowering time: midsummer to early autumn

Planting time: early spring or early to mid autumn

Propagation: take 10 cm (4 in) cuttings in late summer and insert in a peat/sand compost in a cold frame; take 25 cm (10 in) cuttings in mid autumn and insert in a sheltered border outdoors

Pruning: remove dead flower stems; trim hedges in spring

Uses: suitable for low hedges; fragrant flowers and aromatic grey-green foliage – gather blossoms for drying as soon as they come into flower. There are a number of species including the slightly tender *L. stoechas* and many good varieties, 'Hidcote' is especially recommended

Privet

Ligustrum ovalifolium

Site: sun or shade

Soil: ordinary

Height: up to 3.5 m (15 ft)

Spread: up to 3.5 m (15 ft)

Type of shrub: hardy evergreen or semi evergreen

Flowers: cream

Flowering time: early summer to early autumn

Fruits: black berries

Planting time: early to mid spring or mid to late autumn

Propagation: take 30 cm (1 ft) hardwood cuttings in mid autumn and insert them in the garden in a sheltered spot

Pruning: clip hedges when necessary, otherwise allow to grow naturally

Uses: usually grown as a hedge (see page 80); some varieties have attractive foliage variegated with gold

Magnolia

Magnolia × soulangeana

Site: sunny or light shade

Soil: deep rich, lime-free, moist but well drained

Height: up to 3.5 m (15 ft)

Spread: up to 3 m (10 ft)

Type of shrub: hardy, deciduous

Flowers: white flushed with pink, cup shaped

Flowering time: mid spring

Planting time: early to mid spring or autumn

Propagation: sow seeds in mid autumn; layer in early to mid spring; take cuttings of firm young growth in midsummer and insert in a sandy compost with bottom heat; take 30 cm (1 ft) hardwood cuttings in mid autumn and insert in a shady border outdoors

Pruning: none required

Uses: the flowers open before the leaves making a beautiful spring feature in the garden. Several good varieties of this species are available such as 'Lennei' and 'Rustica Rubra'. Also recommended is *M. Kobus*, small white flowers, growing to 12 m (40 ft)

Mahonia

Mahonia

Site: sunny or semi-shade

Soil: rich, well drained

Height: up to 3.75 m (12 ft)

Spread: up to 3.75 m (12 ft)

Type of shrub: hardy evergreen

Flowers: yellow, sweetly scented

Flowering time: early winter to early spring

Fruits: blue-black berries

Planting time: early to mid spring or early to mid autumn

Propagation: sow seeds in late summer; layer in spring or autumn; take 10 cm (4 in) tip cuttings in midsummer and insert in a propagator

Pruning: none required

Uses: the smaller kinds make good ground cover, others are good winter-flowering specimen shrubs. *M. japonica* needs shelter from strong winds, also the good hybrid 'Charity'. Many species and hybrids are available

Mahonia fruits

Crab Apple

Malus

Site: open, sunny

Soil: well drained, enriched with plenty of well-rotted manure or compost

Height: up to 7 m (23 ft)

Spread: up to 4.5 m (15 ft)

Type of tree: hardy, deciduous

Flowers: pink or white

Flowering time: late spring

Fruits: small red or yellow apples

Planting time: late winter to early spring or mid to late autumn

Propagation: sow seeds in spring after stratification; bud on to an apple rootstock in summer; graft on to an apple rootstock in early spring

Pruning: prune in autumn or winter to keep a good shape; thin out congested growth and remove crossing branches

Uses: very decorative specimen tree; fruits can be used for preserving. Many good varieties and species available. Some such as *M. lemoinei* and *M. floribunda* are grown mainly for the beauty of the flowers, others such as 'John Downie', 'Golden Hornet', 'Red Siberian' for their fruits

Prickly Heath

Pernettya mucronata

Site: sunny or light shade

Soil: lime-free, or peaty, moist

Height: up to 1 m (3 ft)

Spread: up to 1 m (3 ft)

Type of shrub: hardy evergreen

Flowers: white

Flowering time: late spring to early summer

Fruits: white, pink, purple or red berries

Planting time: early to late spring or early to late autumn

Propagation: sow seeds in a peaty compost in mid autumn; layer shoots in spring; take 5 cm (2 in) cuttings in autumn and insert in a peat/sand compost; detach rooted suckers in autumn

Pruning: none required

Uses: good berry-bearing ground cover plant. Many varieties are available and it is advisable to plant a mixture to get the best colour effect

Mock Orange

Philadelphus

Site: sun or light shade

Soil: ordinary

Height: up to 3.5 m (12 ft)

Spread: up to 3 m (10 ft)

Type of shrub: hardy, deciduous

Flowers: white, some marked with purple

Flowering time: early and midsummer

Planting time: early spring or mid to late autumn

Propagation: take 10 cm (4 in) cuttings in summer and insert in a peat/sand compost in a cold frame; take 30 cm (1 ft) hardwood cuttings in autumn and insert in a sheltered border outdoors

Pruning: cut back shoots after they have flowered, leave the non-flowering stems

Uses: grown chiefly for the flowers which have a scent like that of orange blossom. Many good species and varieties, some with single flowers such as 'Avalanche', 'Beauclerk', 'Belle Étoile', others with double flowers such as 'Bouquet Blanc', 'Enchantment' and 'Virginal'

Photinia

Photinia villosa

Site: warm, sunny, sheltered

Soil: light, rich, lime-free, well drained

Height: up to 4.5 m (15 ft)

Spread: up to 3 m (10 ft)

Type of shrub: hardy deciduous

Flowers: white

Flowering time: late spring to early summer

Fruits: red berries in autumn

Planting time: early spring or mid to late autumn

Propagation: sow seeds under glass after three months stratification; layer in spring; take 10 cm (4 in) cuttings of side growth in summer and insert in a peat/sand compost

Pruning: none required

Uses: glorious autumn colour, interesting specimen shrub. The evergreen species make good hedges in warm climate areas but these seldom flower or fruit well in cold areas

Phyllodoce

Phyllodoce empetriformis

Site: cool, open

Soil: moist, lime-free, peaty

Height: up to 30 cm (1 ft)

Spread: up to 30 cm (1 ft)

Type of shrub: hardy evergreen

Flowers: reddish-purple, heather-like

Flowering time: late spring to midsummer

Planting time: early to mid spring or early to mid autumn

Propagation: sow seeds in spring; take 5 cm (2 in) cuttings in summer and insert into a peat/sand compost; layer in spring

Pruning: cut off dead flower stems when flowering is over

Uses: good ground cover plant

Pieris

Pieris japonica

Site: sun or semi-shade, shelter from cold winds

Soil: lime-free, fertile

Height: up to 3 m (10 ft)

Spread: up to 3 m (10 ft)

Type of shrub: hardy evergreen

Flowers: white sprays like lily of the valley

Flowering time: early to mid spring

Planting time: early spring or early to mid autumn

Propagation: sow seeds in sandy peat in spring; take 10 cm (4 in) cuttings in late summer and insert them in a sandy compost in a cold frame; layer shoots in autumn

Pruning: remove dead flowers

Uses: very attractive shrub early in the year; leaves are red when young, turning green as they mature. There are other good species and varieties such as 'Forest Flame', *formosa forestii*, and 'Wakehurst'

Shrubby Cinquefoil

Potentilla fruticosa

Site: sunny

Soil: well drained

Height: up to 1.5 m (5 ft)

Spread: up to 1.5 m (5 ft)

Type of shrub: hardy deciduous

Flowers: yellow, white, cream, orange, depending on variety

Flowering time: late spring to late summer

Planting time: early spring or mid to late autumn

Propagation: sow seeds in early spring; take 8 cm (3 in) cuttings with a heel in early autumn and insert in a peat/sand compost in a cold frame

Pruning: in spring shorten shoots by half and remove congested growth

Uses: good ground cover plants, useful in mixed borders on banks and rock gardens. The many varieties include 'Katherine Dykes' primrose yellow, *mandshurica* white, *parvifolia* yellow and 'Tangerine' copper-yellow

Cherry Laurel

Prunus laurocerasus

Site: sun or shade

Soil: ordinary, well drained

Height: up to 6 m (20 ft)

Spread: up to 6 m (20 ft)

Type of shrub: hardy evergreen

Flowers: cream

Flowering time: mid spring

Fruits: red berries turning black

Planting time: mid autumn or early spring

Propagation: sow seeds in summer; take 10 cm (4 in) cuttings with a heel in late summer and insert in a peat/sand compost in a cold frame

Pruning: trim hedges with secateurs in spring or late summer

Uses: useful hedging plant. Very tolerant of shade and drips from overhanging trees. There are a large number of garden varieties

Trim broad-leaved evergreens with secateurs rather than shears to avoid the leaves being cut

Ornamental Peach

Prunus persica 'Klara Mayer'

Site: open, sunny. In cold areas against a wall

Soil: ordinary, well drained

Height: up to 7.5 m (25 ft)

Spread: up to 4.5 m (15 ft)

Type of tree: hardy deciduous

Flowers: pink, double

Flowering time: early to mid spring

Planting time: mid to late autumn or late winter

Propagation: graft in spring onto a *Prunus persica* rootstock; bud in summer onto a *Prunus persica* rootstock

Pruning: none required

Uses: this double-flowered hybrid makes an attractive specimen tree. There are other good forms such as 'Cardinal' red, semi-double, 'Iceberg' white, semi-double, and 'Prince Charming' pinky-red, double

Japanese Cherry

Prunus serrulata

Site: open, sunny or light shade

Soil: ordinary, well drained, preferably containing some lime

Height: up to 7.5 m (25 ft)

Spread: up to 4.5 m (15 ft)

Type of tree: hardy deciduous

Flowers: white, pale pink, pale lemon, single or double according to variety

Flowering time: mid to late spring

Planting time: mid to late autumn or late winter

Propagation: bud onto rootstock of *P. avium* in summer; alternatively graft onto rootstock of *P. avium* in spring

Pruning: none required

Uses: the many garden varieties of this species provide some of the most spectacular of the spring-flowering trees, many also have good autumn colours. 'Amanogawa' with its upright habit is useful for the small garden, others include 'Kanzan', 'Shirofugen' and 'Shirotae'

Mollis Azaleas

Rhododendron

Site: sun or semi-shade

Soil: well drained, lime free, sandy. Dress with peat before planting

Height: up to 2 m (6 ft)

Spread: up to 2 m (6 ft)

Type of shrub: hardy deciduous

Flowers: white, yellow, orange, red or shades of these according to variety

Flowering time: late spring

Planting time: early to mid spring or late summer to late autumn

Propagation: graft or layer onto the common species

Pruning: none required but remove the dead flower heads

Uses: the large blossoms appear before the leaves; colourful shrubs for thin woodland. The many varieties include 'Altaclarense' orange-yellow, 'Comte de Gomer' rose-pink, 'Dr M. Oosthock' orange-red, 'Floradora' orange-red, spotted, 'Mrs Peter Koster' deep red, 'Snowdrift' white and deep yellow

Rhododendron

Rhododendron

Site: light shade

Soil: well drained, lime free, sandy

Height: up to 12 m (40 ft) according to variety

Spread: up to 12 m (40 ft) according to variety

Type of shrub: hardy deciduous or evergreen

Flowers: white, yellow, orange, red, purple according to variety

Flowering time: mid winter to midsummer

Planting time: mid spring

Propagation: take cuttings or graft hardy hybrids; graft or layer deciduous azaleas; grow large-leaved species from seed; take cuttings of alpine species and Kurume azaleas

Pruning: no regular pruning required, remove dead flower heads

Uses: grow well in light shade, can be used as hedges, specimen shrubs or in the mixed border. Hundreds of species and varieties available. They benefit from an annual mulch of peat or other organic matter such as composted bark or leafmould

Staghorn Sumach

Rhus typhina

Site: sunny

Soil: ordinary, well drained

Height: 3 to 4.5 m (10 to 15 ft)

Spread: 3.5 to 5 m (11 to 16 ft)

Type of tree: hardy, deciduous

Flowers: small, red

Flowering time: early to midsummer

Fruits: clusters of crimson hairy fruits

Planting time: mid to late autumn

Propagation: take 10 cm (4 in) heeled cuttings in mid or late summer and insert in a peat/sand compost; detach rooted suckers in autumn and replant at once

Pruning: none required but can be cut back each year in late winter to within 10 cm (4 in) of the main branches to give very large leaves

Uses: spectacular autumn colour and crimson fruits make this a most decorative tree. It can, however, spread rapidly by suckering. 'Laciniata' is a striking form with deeply cut leaves

Flowering Currant

Ribes sanguineum

Site: sun or shade

Soil: ordinary, well drained

Height: 2 to 2.5 m (6 to 8 ft)

Spread: 1.5 to 2 m (5 to 6 ft)

Type of shrub: hardy deciduous

Flowers: red

Flowering time: early to late spring

Fruits: black berries in autumn

Planting time: early spring to mid to late autumn

Propagation: take 25 cm (10 in) hardwood cuttings in autumn and insert outdoors

Pruning: cut out some of the old wood down to ground level in late spring after flowering

Uses: provides good spring colour in the garden and branches are useful in flower arrangements

False Acacia

Robinia pseudoacacia

Site: sunny, sheltered position

Soil: well drained, ordinary

Height: 9 m (30 ft)

Spread: 4.5 m (15 ft)

Type of shrub: hardy deciduous

Flowers: white, pea-like

Flowering time: early summer

Planting time: early spring or mid to late autumn

Propagation: from rooted suckers detached in mid autumn to late winter and plant out immediately: choice kinds by grafting onto R. *pseudoacacia* in spring

Pruning: none required

Uses: as a specimen tree, especially useful in hot, dry places. Tolerant of atmosphere pollution. The illustration is of the form 'Frisia', a very choice kind with golden yellow foliage

Rose

Rosa 'Chicago Peace'

Site: sunny and open

Soil: rich and well drained

Height: 1.2 m (4 ft)

Spread: 1.2 m (4 ft)

Type of rose: hybrid tea

Type of shrub: hardy deciduous

Planting time: mid to late autumn

Propagation: by budding onto a rootstock of a wild rose

Pruning: see illustration below

Uses: as cut flowers

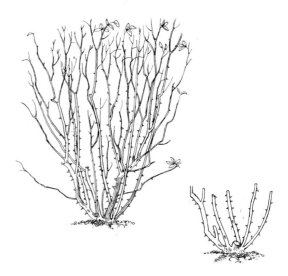

Pruning of a hybrid tea rose: cut out all crossing and diseased wood and reduce remaining stems to one third

Rosa Mundi

Rose gallica 'Versicolor'

Site: sunny and open

Soil: well drained

Height: 1.2 m (4 ft)

Spread: 1.2 m (4 ft)

Type of rose: shrub

Type of shrub: hardy deciduous

Planting time: mid to late autumn

Propagation: take 25 cm (10 in) heeled cuttings in late summer or early autumn, take off all leaves except the top two, insert the base of the cutting into hormone rooting powder and put the cutting out in the garden soil

Pruning: no regular pruning required

Uses: makes a good hedge as it stands hard clipping

Black spot: a fungal disease which affects roses. Spray with a fungicide throughout spring and summer

Willow

Salix

Site: open, sunny or light shade

Soil: ordinary, moist

Height: up to 9 m (30 ft)

Spread: up to 6 m (20 ft)

Type of tree: hardy deciduous

Flowers: silvery-grey male catkins (as in illustration), female flowers are borne on separate trees and are inconspicuous

Flowering time: late winter to late spring

Planting time: early spring or mid to late autumn

Propagation: 25 cm (10 in) hardwood cuttings taken between mid autumn and late winter and planted outside: layer in autumn

Pruning: no regular pruning: those with coloured stems should be cut down almost to ground level (or to within 5 cm [2 in] of the main branches) in late winter to ensure the stems remain a brilliant colour

Uses: twigs bearing catkins are good in early spring flower arrangements. The coloured-barked kinds such as *S. alba* 'Chermesina' provide interesting winter colour; lovely specimen trees

Clematis
Clematis

Site: sunny walls, roots in shade

Soil: deep, well drained, do well on chalk

Height: 3 to 12 m (10 to 40 ft)

Type of plant: hardy and half-hardy, deciduous or evergreen, climbing by means of 'tendrils'

Flowers: all colours

Flowering time: mid spring to mid autumn

Planting time: autumn or spring

Propagation: sow seeds in spring; take cuttings in spring or summer; layer in summer

Species cultivated: there is a large range offered including *C. montana* (photograph) vigorous, deciduous, white or pink flowers in spring; *armandii* vigorous, evergreen, white spring flowers, and many other species and garden hybrids

Pruning: the early summer flowerers should be lightly pruned in late winter. The late-flowering kinds can be pruned at the same time but these should be cut back more severely. Clematis which flower over a long season should be lightly pruned; early flowering kinds immediately after flowering

Cultivation and uses: mulch well in spring. Give firm support. Disturb roots as little as possible and do not transplant. Water well in dry weather

Cup-and-saucer Vine
Cobaea

Site: sunny, warm walls or trellises; sunny cool greenhouse. Only likely to survive outdoors for any length of time in a frost-free climate

Soil: light

Height: 3 to 6 m (10 to 20 ft)

Type of plant: half-hardy, fast-growing climber, usually grown as an annual

Flowers: purple and white

Flowering time: late summer to early autumn

Sowing time: spring

Planting time: as soon as frosts are passed; in warm climates as soon as plants are large enough

Propagation: sow seeds in 15 to 18°C (59 to 64°F). Variegated variety by cuttings taken in summer and rooted in a propagator

Species cultivated: *C. scandens*, purple and white flowers, also a white form 'Alba'

Cultivation and uses: water well in dry weather. Provides fast, decorative cover

Fishbone Cotoneaster
Cotoneaster horizontalis

Site: sun or shade

Soil: ordinary

Height: 1 to 1.25 m (3 to 4 ft)

Spread: 1 to 1.25 m (3 to 4 ft)

Type of plant: deciduous shrub

Flowers: small, whitish-pink; followed by abundant red berries

Flowering time: summer

Sowing time: spring

Planting time: autumn to late winter

Propagation: sow seeds outdoors after they have been stratified; take cuttings in summer and root in a propagator or take hardwood cuttings in autumn

Species cultivated: *C. horizontalis* (photograph) and several good forms including 'Variegatus' with cream-variegated leaves

Pruning: no regular pruning required, if necessary cut back in late winter

Cultivation and uses: good autumn colour; useful for shaded walls or those subject to cold winds. *C. franchetti* and *C. lacteus* are other species which make good wall cover

Ivy
Hedera

Site: sun or shade

Soil: ordinary

Height: will cover anything eventually, fairly fast growing

Type of plant: hardy evergreen climbing shrub

Flowers: insignificant, green, followed by black, orange or yellow berries

Planting time: spring or autumn

Planting distance: 60 cm (2 ft)

Propagation: take cuttings and root outdoors in autumn or in a propagator in spring or summer; layer shoots at any time

Species cultivated: recommended are *H. canariensis* and its variety 'Variegata', large leathery leaves in grey, green and white; *H. helix* and its many varieties with leaves in a range of shades and shapes; *H. colchica*, largest of all ivies, and its varieties 'Dentata Variegata' green, grey and cream and 'Sulphur Heart' (photograph)

Pruning: prune in spring, cutting out straggly shoots

Cultivation and uses: tolerant of difficult sites and atmospheric pollution. Climbs by means of aerial roots. Can be grown in pots to make effective house plants but only for cool rooms

Hop
Humulus

Site: sunny

Soil: deep, well manured

Height: 3 to 4.5 m (10 to 15 ft)

Type of plant: hardy herbaceous perennial climber

Flowers: male and female flowers carried on separate plants; the female flowers are the hops of commerce and female plants are the more decorative

Flowering time: summer

Sowing time: early spring

Planting time: late winter or early spring

Propagation: sow seeds in early spring in 15 to 18°C (59 to 64°F) or sow outdoors in late spring; divide in spring

Species cultivated: *H. japonicus*, Japanese hop, can be grown as an annual from seeds and planted out in late spring; *H. lupulus*, hop, and variety 'Aureus' (photograph) with golden leaves

Pruning: cut plants down in autumn

Cultivation and uses: mulch with decayed manure or garden compost in spring. Water well in dry weather. Good for providing summer cover

Hydrangea
Hydrangea

Site: sunny or semi-shaded walls or trees

Soil: fairly rich, moisture-retentive

Height: 15 m (50 ft)

Type of plant: hardy deciduous, vigorous climbing

Flowers: creamy white blooms carried in flat clusters

Flowering time: summer

Planting time: autumn or spring

Propagation: take cuttings in summer and insert in pots of sand and peat in a frame or greenhouse

Species cultivated: *H. petiolaris* (photograph) self clinging by means of aerial roots

Pruning: cut away dead or straggly shoots in spring

Cultivation and uses: topdress every year with decayed manure or garden compost. Very tolerant of most climatic conditions

Morning Glory, Convolvulus
Ipomoea

Site: sunny, sheltered walls or trellises. In cooler climates usually grown as annuals and discarded at the end of the growing season

Soil: ordinary, light

Height: 1.25 to 4.25 m (4 to 12 ft)

Type of plant: half-hardy annual and perennial twining plants

Flowers: blue, purple, pink or white, some bi-coloured, funnel shaped

Flowering time: midsummer to early autumn

Planting time: when danger of frost is past in cooler climates, spring in warmer climates

Planting distance: 30 cm (12 in)

Propagation: sow seeds in 15 to 18°C (59 to 64°F) in spring. Pot on singly and plant out. Seeds may be soaked for 24 hours in water before sowing

Species cultivated: *I. purpurea*, half-hardy annual, climbs vigorously to 3 m (10 ft), purple flowers; *I quamoclit*, half-hardy annual climbing to 2 m (6 ft), red and yellow flowers; *I. tricolor* (photograph) half-hardy perennial growing to 2.5 m (8 ft), reddish purple to blue flowers

Pruning: remove flower heads as they fade to prolong the flowering season

Cultivation and uses: no special requirements. Can be grown in large containers

Jasmine
Jasminum

Site: sunny walls or trellis; *J. nudiflorum* also in partial shade

Soil: good, well drained

Height: 2 m (6 ft) upwards

Type of plant: hardy deciduous climbers and tender evergreen climbers

Flowers: white or yellow

Flowering time: winter and spring, summer

Planting time: autumn or late winter

Propagation: cuttings inserted in a propagator in summer for tender kinds, or in frames in late summer or autumn for hardy kinds. Layer shoots in spring or summer

Species cultivated: the two hardy recommended species are *J. nudiflorum* (photograph), deciduous, yellow, winter flowering and *J. officinale*, deciduous, white fragrant flowers in summer. Two good tender sorts are *J. polyanthum*, evergreen, with fragrant white flowers in winter and spring and *J. mesnyi*, evergreen, with yellow semi-double spring flowers

Pruning: most kinds only need thinning out if overgrown. Prune *J. nudiflorum* after flowering, cutting the shoots that have flowered back to 5 or 8 cm (2 or 3 in) of the base

Cultivation and uses: the tender sorts grow outdoors in warm climates but require greenhouse protection elsewhere

Honeysuckle

Lonicera

Site: cool and shaded for the roots, sun or part shade for top growth. Tender kinds in a frost-proof greenhouse in the cooler climates

Soil: ordinary, well drained

Height: up to 9 m (30 ft)

Type of plant: hardy; deciduous or evergreen

Flowers: yellow, orange, red or crimson

Flowering time: early summer to early autumn and late autumn to spring

Planting time: deciduous kinds in autumn or late winter, evergreen kinds in spring or autumn

Propagation: take cuttings in summer and insert in a propagator; take hardwood cuttings in autumn, layer in spring or autumn and then sow out of doors

Species cultivated: *L. periclymenum* (photograph) cream and purple, scented, summer to autumn, deciduous, to 6 m (20 ft); *L. japonica* creamy white, scented, summer, evergreen, to 9 m (30 ft) and varieties; *L. aureoreticulata* with green leaves netted with yellow

Cultivation and uses: prune by cutting out some of the older stems after flowering. Mulch in spring. Less likely to be attacked by aphids if planted in a shaded position

Virginia Creeper, Vines

Parthenocissus

Site: sun or light shade against walls or on pergolas, fences

Soil: ordinary, containing decayed manure or garden compost

Height: up to 21 m (70 ft)

Type of plant: hardy or slightly tender deciduous self-clinging climbers

Flowers: insignificant, mostly green followed by small blackish fruits

Flowering time: late spring, early summer

Planting time: autumn or late winter

Propagation: layer shoots in spring or autumn; take half-ripe cuttings in summer or hardwood cuttings in autumn; sow seeds in a frame or cold greenhouse in autumn

Species cultivated: *P. henryana*, bright green leaves with silver and pink variegations, to 9 m (30 ft), slightly tender; *P. quinquefolia*, to 21 m (70 ft), brilliant autumn colouring; *P. tricuspidata* (photograph), Boston Ivy, to 15 m (50 ft)

Pruning: remove overcrowded or unwanted growth in summer. Pinch out tips of young plants

Cultivation and uses: choose a sheltered site for the slightly tender kinds. No additional support needed once the plants are established. Noted for their autumn colouring

Plumbago, Cape Leadwort
Plumbago

Site: in cooler climates: outdoors in a sunny sheltered position in summer and in a frostproof greenhouse in winter. In frost-free climates; outdoors all the year round, sunny

Soil: good, moist

Height: to 4.5 m (15 ft)

Type of plant: half-hardy evergreen climber

Flowers: pale blue or white

Flowering time: summer

Planting time: summer in cool climates, late winter or spring in frost-free climates

Propagation: take cuttings of non-flowering shoots in summer or sow seeds in a greenhouse in spring

Species cultivated: *P. capensis* (photograph) is the recommended species and there is a white variety 'Alba'

Pruning: shorten growths made in the previous year to a few inches in late winter

Cultivation and uses: tie stems regularly to a supporting framework. Water well in spring and summer. When grown in pots in the greenhouse use a good potting compost and maintain a winter minimum of 7 C (45 F). Feed in summer and keep fairly dry in winter

Russian Vine
Polygonum

Site: sun or partial shade, will quickly cover trellises, walls or trees

Soil: ordinary, any type

Height: to 12 m (40 ft), can grow 3 to 4.5 m (10 to 15 ft) in a year

Type of plant: hardy, vigorous, deciduous twiner

Flowers: white or pinkish

Flowering time: summer

Planting time: autumn or spring

Propagation: layer shoots in late spring or early summer; take hardwood cuttings in autumn

Species cultivated: *P. aubertii* (photograph) white flowers in late summer and autumn; *P. baldschuanicum*, pinkish-white flowers in late summer and autumn

Pruning: none required but pinch out the tips of young plants to encourage branching

Cultivation and uses: useful for covering unsightly garden buildings or old tree stumps. No special requirements

Firethorn
Pyracantha

Site: part shade or full sun

Soil: ordinary, well drained

Height: to 6 m (20 ft) depending on species

Spread: to 4.5 m (15 ft) depending on species

Type of plant: hardy evergreen shrub with spiny branches

Flowers: clusters of white flowers followed by red, yellow or orange berries

Flowering time: early summer, berries from autumn through winter

Planting time: spring or autumn

Propagation: sow seeds in spring; take half-ripe cuttings in summer or early autumn

Species cultivated: many available, typical are *P. angustifolia*, orange-yellow berries; *P. atalantioides*, scarlet berries; *P. coccinea*, red berries; *P. rogersiana*, reddish orange berries and variety 'Flava' with yellow berries; 'Orange Glow' (photograph) orange-red berries

Pruning: remove badly placed shoots after flowering but take care not to cut out any shoots on which berries are starting to form

Cultivation and uses: can be trained as climbers by tying in growths to supporting wires. Does not transplant well, buy container-grown plants to avoid root breakage

Wisteria
Wisteria

Site: sunny sheltered walls, trained to wires or trellises

Soil: rich, good

Height: to 18 m (60 ft)

Type of plant: hardy deciduous climbing shrub

Flowers: mauve, lilac, blue, pink or white in long trails

Flowering time: late spring to early summer

Planting time: spring

Propagation: layer shoots after flowering; take half-ripe cuttings in summer or autumn

Species cultivated: *W. sinensis*, Chinese wisteria, deep lilac, scented, 12 to 18 m (40 to 60 ft), and its varieties; *W. floribunda*, Japanese wisteria, violet-blue, scented, to 6 m (20 ft), and its varieties

Pruning: prune regularly, shortening side shoots to four or five leaves in summer and cutting back further if required to 5 or 8 cm (2 or 3 in) in late winter. Large plants need not be pruned

Cultivation and uses: tie growths into the supports until plants are growing well. No special requirements

Ornamental Conifers

Conifers are trees and shrubs which carry cones of one sort or another and mostly have narrow, rather thickened leaves. Most are evergreen and retain their foliage all the year round but some, such as metasequoia and larch, are deciduous.

There is nothing new about the use of conifers in gardens, but what is certainly noteworthy is that better use is now being made of them as design features in their own right. For a start, they have a wide range of shapes and leaf textures and often the most appealing colourings, in shades of green, grey, yellow and blue. Gradually, too, more forms of the various genera are being introduced which offer even more exciting possibilities. Conifers generally have much to offer the gardener with the imagination to use them well.

It is in winter that conifers really come into their own for their colourings and textures are strongly contrasted with the bare outlines of deciduous trees and shrubs. When considering them for certain garden sites this thought should be kept in mind.

Culturally, and particularly with regard to planting, they need the same kind of treatment as evergreen trees and shrubs (see my recommendation on p. 10), but I would emphasise again the importance of giving them every care and attention in the crucial time between planting and full re-establishment.

Where they differ from ordinary evergreens is in their vulnerability to snow damage, their close-knit branches acting as a perfect snow trap in blizzard conditions. Branches loaded down in this way need to be relieved of their burden with the least possible delay before permanent damage is done.

Golden-foliaged conifers will, as a rule, only colour up really well if they are exposed to plenty of sunshine, so that is something to bear in mind when finding them homes. Their warm colouring can do much to enliven the garden at all times of the year.

One of the most exciting horticultural 'finds' of recent times has been the dawn redwood, *Metasequoia glypto-stroboides*, which dates back to the fossil age and is one of that very rare breed, a deciduous conifer. It was re-discovered in its native China in the early 1940's. This is described on p. 70, and it is worth pointing out that although it is proving to be a tree of great height (and fast growth) it can still be accommodated in gardens of medium size as its spread is relatively modest.

An aspect of conifer utilisation which should never be overlooked is the highly effective background they can provide for garden trees and large shrubs which flower in the leafless state and thus often need a rather dark background to throw them into relief. Perhaps the best example of such a tree is the popular winter-flowering cherry, *Prunus subhirtella autumnalis*, which bears its white, semi-double flowers intermittently right through from late autumn to the start of spring. Again, the witch hazels like *Hamamelis mollis* and its varieties can gain enormously in this respect, their curious flowers with yellow strap-like petals benefiting greatly from the contrast.

Planting and aftercare

But let us return for a moment to more practical matters, and that hazardous post-planting period. Even more than ordinary evergreens, conifers can suffer from the effects of drying winds, so, whenever possible (and certainly with valuable specimen plants) erect a temporary screen of hessian on the windward side. This screen must be well secured with stakes and should be slightly taller than the plant or, if the plant is small enough, a polythene bag can be put right over it and secured around the stem. All types of protection should be removed in spring.

Methods of planting are shown on page 11.

Again, as with other trees and shrubs, be sure to watch the water position in the spring and summer following planting, conifers should never be allowed to dry out at the roots or their growth will be seriously retarded. It is a good idea to spray the foliage over with clear water each evening if dry weather follows planting as this helps to keep down moisture loss from the leaves until the roots are fully established.

I always consider that a mulch is very beneficial to newly planted shrubs and this also applies to the conifers. Mulching quite simply means spreading a layer of some form of organic matter such as garden compost, peat, leafmould or manure over the soil around the plant keeping it away from the stem. Mulches have the effect of conserving the moisture in the soil.

Unless they are grown as hedges, conifers do not require any pruning. However, occasionally one branch may grow out of proportion to the rest of the tree and so will need cutting back, or a prostrate form may become too invasive and have to be curbed. Any pruning required can be done at almost any time of the year but if there is a choice of season then summer or autumn are the best because the plants will lose less of their sap, or resin, at these times.

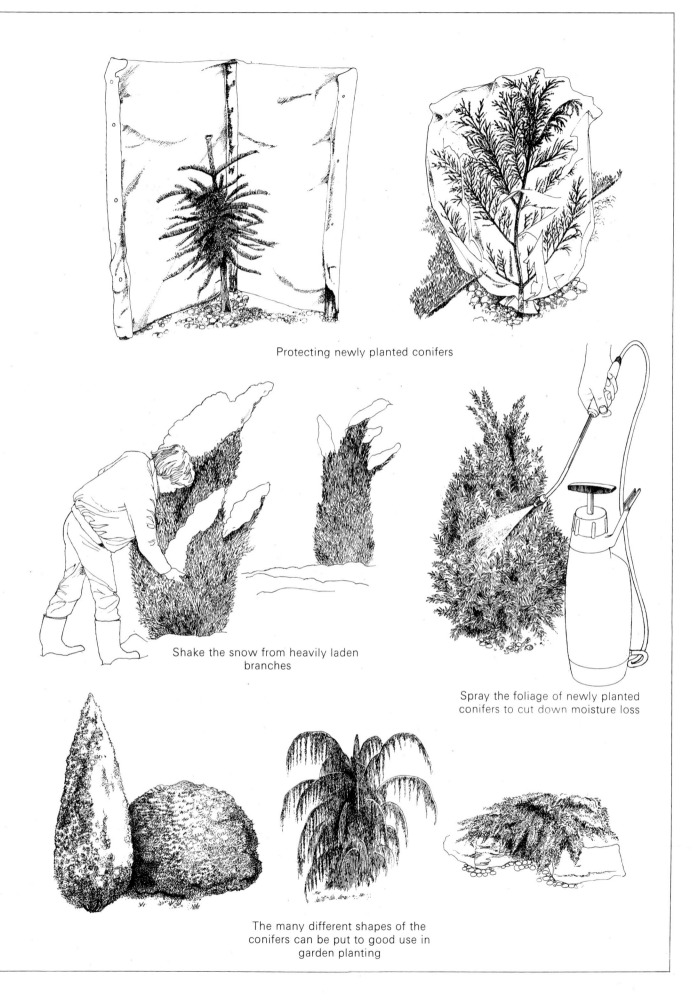

Protecting newly planted conifers

Shake the snow from heavily laden
branches

Spray the foliage of newly planted
conifers to cut down moisture loss

The many different shapes of the
conifers can be put to good use in
garden planting

Monkey Puzzle
Araucaria

Site: sheltered

Soil: deep, fertile and moisture retentive

Height: 15 to 25 m (50 to 80 ft)

Spread: 4.5 to 6 m (15 to 20 ft)

Foliage: long, scaly branches sweep gracefully down from the central trunk which is also clad with the spiny scales in the first years of growth

Planting time: spring or autumn

Propagation: sow seeds under glass, 18°C (65°F), in spring

Recommended species: *A. araucana* (photograph) (syn: *A. imbricata*) is the only species which is hardy outdoors in this country

Cultivation and uses: this tree should be given plenty of room and grown as an individual specimen if it is to be seen at its best; on poor soils the branches tend to turn brown and drop their scales more quickly than if given a cool, moist root run; the removal of faded branches will improve the tree's appearance; the best trees will be seen in the mildest parts of the country

Cedar
Cedrus

Site: open or sheltered

Soil: deep, fertile and well drained, but not dry

Height: 25 to 36 m (80 to 120 ft)

Spread: up to 9 m (up to 30 ft and more)

Foliage: short needles which give the tree a fluffy appearance. The branches are either gracefully sweeping or almost horizontal

Planting time: spring or autumn

Propagation: sow seeds outdoors as soon as they are available

Recommended species: *C. atlantica*, Mount Atlas cedar, with sweeping branches which are especially effective in the blue-grey variety *glauca*; *C. libani*, cedar of Lebanon, horizontal, fresh green branches which have the appearance of grassy mounds; *C. deodara*, the deodar (photograph), has an elegant branch network and pendulous shoot tips

Cultivation and uses: among the most majestic of conifers, the cedars should be given plenty of room and planted where their form can be appreciated from a distance; they are by no means suitable for small gardens where they will soon take over and cut out light from nearby house windows

Lawson Cypress
Chamaecyparis lawsoniana

Site: open or partially shaded

Soil: fertile and moisture retentive

Height: up to 40 m (135 ft)

Spread: up to 4.5 m (15 ft)

Foliage: dusky green foliage, neat and scaly

Planting time: spring or autumn

Propagation: take cuttings of healthy young growths in summer or autumn and root in a warm propagator

Recommended species: *C. lawsoniana* has a number of attractive varieties: 'Allumii' blue grey foliage; 'Columnaris' conical; 'Ellwoodii' feathery grey green foliage; 'Pottenii' columnar, soft feathery foliage

Cultivation and uses: little is needed in the way of cultivation once the plants have become established; they make good specimens and *C. lawsoniana* itself can be used as a hedging plant, see page 77

If shrubs arrive when the ground is unsuitable for planting, heel them in in a sheltered part of the garden

Hinoki Cypress
Chamaecyparis obtusa

Site: open or partially shaded

Soil: fertile and moisture retentive

Height: up to 7 m (23 ft)

Spread: up to 3 m (10 ft)

Foliage: neat, scaly, typical 'cypress' type

Planting time: spring or autumn

Propagation: take cuttings of healthy young growths in summer or autumn and root in a warm propagator

Recommended species: this species is mostly seen in its dwarf varieties *nana gracilis* (photograph) which has dark green fans of foliage, and *nana aurea* which is tinged with yellow

Cultivation and uses: little is needed in the way of cultivation once the plants have become established; they are all slow growers; the dwarf kinds make good rock garden plants

Sawara Cypress

Chamaecyparis pisifera

Site: open or partially shaded

Soil: reasonably fertile and moisture retentive

Height: up to 9 m (30 ft)

Spread: up to 4.5 m (15 ft)

Foliage: fern-like sprays with silver markings underneath; resinous odour

Planting time: spring or autumn

Propagation: take cuttings of healthy young growths in summer or autumn and root in a warm propagator

Recommended species: usually the smaller varieties of this species are grown like *filifera aurea*, golden with drooping branches; *plumosa* with green and feathery foliage; *plumosa aurea* (photograph) yellow-tipped feathery foliage; 'Squarrosa' spreading, upswept branches of blue-grey foliage, suitable for ground cover

Cultivation and uses: little is needed in the way of cultivation once the plants are established; all varieties are slow growing; the dwarfer kinds make good rock garden plants

Maidenhair Tree

Ginkgo

Site: open and sunny

Soil: fertile and well drained

Height: 18 to 30 m (60 to 100 ft)

Spread: up to 8 m (up to 25 ft)

Foliage: beautiful fan-shaped leaves which are similar in appearance to those of the maidenhair fern. Although green during the summer, the leaves turn yellow before being shed in autumn. This tree is one of the few deciduous conifers

Planting time: autumn or late winter

Propagation: sow seeds in sandy soil in a cold frame as soon as they are available; cuttings can be rooted in a propagating frame in summer

Recommended species: *G. biloba* (photograph) is the only species but it has two varieties: *fastigiata*, in which the branches are more upright than normal, and *pendula*, which has a weeping habit

Cultivation and uses: this is a highly ornamental tree which should be grown as an isolated specimen; male and female forms are available and the male is preferable as the female produces foul-smelling fruits; a good tree for autumn colour

Chinese Juniper

Juniperus chinensis

Site: open and sunny

Soil: ordinary

Height: up to 6 m (20 ft)

Spread: up to 1.5 m (5 ft)

Foliage: dark green; adult foliage consists of closely-pressed scales; juvenile foliage is bigger and prickly

Planting time: spring or autumn

Propagation: take cuttings of healthy young shoots in autumn and root them in a cold frame

Recommended species: *J. chinensis* has a number of varieties including *aurea* bright yellow; 'Blue Point' blue-grey foliage and upright growth; 'Pfitzeriana' (photograph) has a flatter habit of growth and a spreading form

Cultivation and uses: once established these plants will grow freely without further trouble; make good specimens especially in the rock garden; spreading forms can be used for ground cover

Common Juniper

Juniperus communis

Site: open and sunny

Soil: ordinary

Height: up to 3 m (10 ft)

Spread: up to 5 m (16 ft)

Foliage: grey-green juvenile leaves

Planting time: spring or autumn

Propagation: take cuttings of healthy young shoots in autumn and root in a cold frame

Recommended species: there are a number of varieties of *J. communis* including the following: *compressa* (photograph) an upright plant; *depressa aurea* a prostrate yellow-foliaged form

Cultivation and uses: once established these plants will grow freely without further trouble; the upright forms make good focal points in the rock garden; they are all slow growing

Larch
Larix

Site: open and sunny

Soil: ordinary, well drained

Height: up to 30 m (up to 100 ft)

Spread: 3 to 6 m (10 to 20 ft)

Foliage: soft bright green needles which turn yellow before being shed in autumn. A deciduous conifer

Planting time: autumn

Propagation: place seed in pots between layers of sand and allow to stand in a cold frame for three months; after this time sow on a soil mixture in the frame

Recommended species: *L. decidua* is the European larch and makes a tree between 15 and 30 m (50 and 100 ft) high; *L. kaempferi* (photograph), the Japanese Larch is slightly smaller and has broader needles and longer branches

Cultivation and uses: little attention is needed after planting, though dead branches may be cut out when necessary; larches may be planted in groups, where they will produce an open canopy under which woodland plants can thrive, or singly as specimen trees

Dawn Redwood
Metasequoia

Site: open and sunny

Soil: fertile and moisture retentive

Height: up to 30 m (up to 100 ft)

Spread: up to 3 m (up to 10 ft)

Foliage: rich green fronds that turn orange before they fall in autumn; one of the few deciduous conifers

Planting time: autumn or late winter

Propagation: sow seed outdoors as soon as available; root cuttings of firm young growths in a propagating frame in summer

Recommended species: *M. glyptostroboides* (photograph) is the only species

Cultivation and uses: a superb plant for moist soil, the dawn redwood makes a good specimen tree with spectacular autumn tints

Norway Spruce Christmas Tree
Picea abies

Site: open or partially shady

Soil: deep, rich and moist

Height: up to 20 m (65 ft)

Spread: up to 6 m (20 ft)

Foliage: stiff needles borne on the upper side of the branch only

Planting time: autumn or late winter

Propagation: sow seeds outdoors in sandy soil as soon as available; take cuttings of firm young growths in summer and root in a propagating frame

Recommended species: *P. abies* has several dwarf forms; 'Clanbrassilliana' (photograph) 30 cm (1 ft) a slow-growing type which forms a dome and produces bright green buds in winter; 'Gregoryana' 15 to 20 cm (6 to 8 in) similar but even smaller; *pumila nigra* 20 to 30 cm (8 to 12 in) tall and up to 2 m (6 ft) across, dark green foliage, slow growing

Cultivation and uses: the taller-growing varieties make good specimen trees which offer year-round interest; the dwarfer types are excellent plants for the rock garden where they make eye-catching features

Canadian Spruce
Picea glauca

Site: open or partially shady

Soil: deep, rich and moist

Height: up to 8 m (26 ft)

Spread: up to 2 m (6 ft)

Foliage: narrow grey-green needles surrounding the branch

Planting time: autumn or late winter

Propagation: sow seeds outdoors in sandy soil as soon as available; take cuttings of firm young growths in summer and root in a propagating frame

Recommended species: *P. glauca* has several dwarf varieties including *albertiana conica* (photograph) which is 60 to 100 cm (2 to 3 ft) and forms an upright conical tree with light green needles; *nana* grows up to 70 cm (28 in) and has grey-blue needles

Cultivation and uses: the taller-growing *P. glauca* makes a good specimen tree; the dwarfer types are excellent plants for the rock garden where they make eye-catching features

Mountain Pine

Pinus mugo

Site: open or partially shaded

Soil: ordinary, well drained

Height: up to 3 m (10 ft)

Spread: up to 3 m (10 ft)

Foliage: large needles borne in pairs

Planting time: autumn or late winter

Propagation: sow seeds outdoors in sandy soil as soon as they are available

Recommended species: *P. mugo* has a dwarf variety *pumilio* (photograph), the dwarf mountain, both are shrubby in habit and do not have a central trunk

Cultivation and uses: pines will tolerate a wide range of conditions and *P. mugo* is happy in coastal districts swept by salt winds; it is suitable for growing on ledges and in the rock garden

Weymouth Pine

Pinus strobus

Site: open or partially shaded

Soil: ordinary, well drained

Height: up to 25 m (80 ft)

Spread: up to 4.5 m (15 ft)

Foliage: dark bluish green needles arranged in whorls

Planting time: autumn or late winter

Propagation: sow seeds outdoors in sandy soil as soon as they are available

Recommended species: *P. strobus* has a number of varieties; *nana* (photograph) is lower growing than the species and forms a bush; 'Fastigiata' is an upright column with erect-growing branches; 'Pendula' is a weeping form

Cultivation and uses: pines will tolerate a wide range of conditions; tall varieties make good specimen trees and lower growing plants are suitable for the rock garden

Yew
Taxus

Site: sunny or quite heavily shaded

Soil: ordinary, deep, well drained

Height: up to 15 m (50 ft) in time

Spread: up to 6 m (20 ft)

Foliage: narrow leaves, usually dark green but sometimes golden yellow, carried on horizontal or upright branches. Red berries are carried in autumn

Planting time: spring or autumn

Propagation: take cuttings of firm young growths in summer and root in a propagating frame

Recommended species: *T. baccata* (photograph) Common Yew, is the tallest-growing species, up to 15 m (50 ft), and it carries the well-known dark green leaves. Its variety *fastigiata* is the Irish Yew – an upright plant which does not grow quite so tall. *T.b. fastigiata aurea* is a particularly attractive slow-growing variety with golden yellow foliage and upright branches. Dwarfer varieties include: *T.b. repens aurea*, 1 to 1.25 m (3 to 4 ft), prostrate with golden foliage, and *T.b. standishii*, also golden yellow, but forming a narrow column up to 1.25 m (4 ft) high

Cultivation and uses: yews are very long-lived trees and although they may be very large they take quite some time to reach their full size; miniature forms are best planted on the rock garden and the taller forms can be planted as isolated specimens or clipped into decorative shapes; yew is a particularly good hedge plant but it is poisonous to cattle and horses and should not be grown where these animals have access. See also page 81

Arbor-Vitae
Thuja

Site: sunny or partially shady

Soil: ordinary, well drained

Height: up to 30 m, (100 ft), though the garden kinds listed below are considerably smaller

Spread: up to 3 or 4.5 m (10 or 15 ft)

Foliage: scaly and similar to that of the False Cypress but usually more shiny

Planting time: autumn or spring.

Propagation: take cuttings of firm young growths in summer and root in a propagator

Recommended species: *T. occidentalis* is an excellent species for gardens if grown in the following varieties: 'Rheingold' (photograph), 1.25 m (4 ft), yellow, tightly packed fans of growth; 'Danica', 45 cm (18 in), a rounded green dome becoming bronze in winter; 'Smaragd', 2 to 2.5 m (6 to 8 ft), pyramidal with rich green foliage, good for hedging. *T. orientalis* also has some good varieties including: *aurea nana*, 60 to 75 cm (2 to 2½ ft), forming a golden-yellow egg-shaped bush; and *elegantissima*, 1.25 to 1.5 m (4 to 5 ft), columnar with yellow furnish which is burnished bronze in winter; *T. plicata* is the western red cedar, an enormous tree better cultivated in its varieties *zebrina*, variegated with creamy yellow, and growing less vigorously; and 'Stoneham Gold', 1 m (3 ft), yellow foliage

Cultivation and uses: once established these plants require little attention; the taller varieties make good focal points in the garden and can also be grown as hedges and windbreaks; the smaller kinds are ideal for the rock garden. See also page 81

Hedges

You could say that it is the professional gardener coming out in me, but there are few things that I like to see more than a beautifully trimmed hedge – say of hawthorn (of which I've a long stretch in my garden) or the excellent Leyland cypress, *Cupressocyparis leylandii*, which I've also put to good use.

So many shrubs and trees lend themselves to hedging purposes that it requires a lot of clear thought before deciding what to put at the end of the garden, perhaps to provide privacy or the kind of shelter which makes it possible to grow many plants more successfully.

You will find useful suggestions on the pages which follow. In particular, I would draw your attention to those shrubs which make attractive and efficient informal hedges for gardens of reasonable size. Things like the handsome barberries, *Berberis* × *stenophylla* and *B. darwinii* – the first with deep yellow flowers and the second with orange flowers in spring – which will make hedges of 1.5 to 2 m (5 to 6 ft) or a little more in height; and the firethorns – the various species of pyracantha with their white flowers followed by glowing berries.

If an impenetrable screen is required you may turn to the barberries or, even more likely, the versatile hawthorn, *Crataegus monogyna*, which you can have from head height to 4.5 m (15 ft) or more, if that is what is needed.

Siting

A few points to remember when choosing the site for your hedge are: (1) that you will need access to both sides if clipping is necessary; (2) if it is a boundary hedge it should not encroach on your neighbour's property; (3) hedges cast shade and take food and moisture from the soil so it is not a good idea to have a flower border immediately beside them – lawns or paths are a better choice.

Preparation for planting

Whatever kind of hedge you have in mind there are basic cultural attentions which must be given due heed, simply because a hedge will be in position for a very long time and good soil preparation is all important. Once it is planted you can do little about getting the soil in good heart in a structural sense, and it is important that this should be done in advance – just as it is wise to make sure that soil drainage is adequate.

Most important, think ahead and get this basic work done well in advance of planting. What you need to do is to prepare a strip at least 1 m (3 ft) wide along the planting line. Normally, it will be sufficient to cultivate this to a depth of a spade's blade, lining the bottom of the trench with humus-forming material as digging proceeds – this could be well-rotted farmyard manure (best of all) garden compost, leafmould, peat or something like spent hops – but if the soil is on the heavy side and therefore not all that free-draining then I would certainly advise double-digging, which means digging to twice the depth of the

spade's blade with the sub-soil being left in the same relative position as before. This is quite a laborious task but it could, in such circumstances, pay dividends in the years to come.

With digging completed, and some weeks in advance of planting, fork a dressing of bonemeal into the surface soil at the rate of about 110 g per sq m (4 oz to the sq yd); this slow-release phosphatic fertiliser will aid root formation which is most important.

Planting

If the hedging plant of your choice needs planting at a distance of 45 cm (18 in) or less then I would advise taking out a trench 38 to 45 cm (15 to 18 in) wide. Hawthorn and privet fall in this category, for instance, while *Cupressocyparis leylandii* and the thujas are outside it. With these last, and many others, it is best to prepare individual planting holes at the required spacing.

Preparing the planting holes differs in no way from the procedure outlined on p. 10 for planting individual shrubs, but to get the spacing even I would suggest marking out the planting stations with canes before you start. Make sure that the holes are of such a size that the plant's roots can be accommodated at their full spread. Fill in around the roots with good soil, and always plant firmly. Wind-rock is a menace to shrubs trying to establish themselves, and it may be necessary to stake the plants individually or to tie them to wires strained between stout posts at each end of the hedge. After planting, water thoroughly and continue watering for a few weeks if the weather is dry.

Trimming

To look at their best hedges must be correctly cared for. With formal hedges (those which are kept clipped) that means regular trimming at the right time of year. With informal hedges (those allowed to grow naturally) it means little more than cutting back occasionally any growths which get too much out of line. Electric trimmers are now used very widely, but if you make do with hedge trimmers do ensure that these are kept sharp – it makes an enormous difference to the effort needed to work along a stretch of hedge. Again, large-leaved evergreens should really be cut back with secateurs so that you don't end up with a lot of sliced up and disfigured leaves; but, of course, it is time-consuming. When using hedge trimmers or shears, hold them so that the blades lie flat against the surface to be cut.

General care

Hedges need feeding just like any other plant and you should take care not to dig the ground around them as this will disturb many of their roots. Feed in spring with a compound fertiliser lightly sprinkled over the soil on each side of the hedge and mulch with well-rotted manure, garden compost or other organic matter if possible.

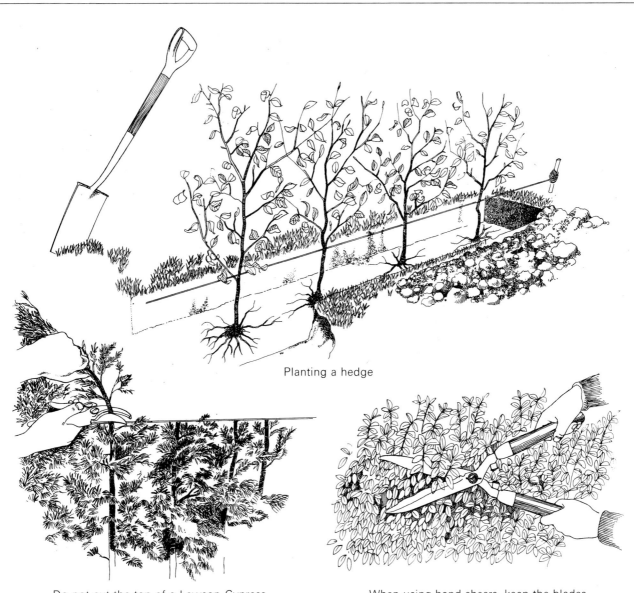

Planting a hedge

Do not cut the top of a Lawson Cypress hedge until it has grown beyond the required height

When using hand shears, keep the blades flat against the hedge

Powered hedge trimmers make the job of hedge clipping much easier

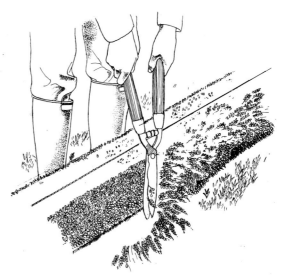

Clipping a low box hedge with hand shears

Barberry
Berberis

Site: sun or light shade

Soil: well drained, good on sandy or chalky soils

Height: up to 3 m (10 ft)

Type of plant: hardy evergreen and deciduous shrubs

Planting time: deciduous kinds in autumn or late winter; evergreen kinds in spring or early autumn

Planting distance: 38 to 60 cm (15 to 24 in) apart depending on height of species

Propagation: take heeled cuttings in late summer and insert in pots of sandy soil; layer shoots in spring

Species cultivated: *B. darwinii*, evergreen, to 2.5 m (8 ft), yellow flowers followed by blue-black berries; *B. thunbergii atropurpurea* (photograph), to 120 cm (4 ft), colourful foliage, red and yellow flowers, red berries, deciduous; *B. × stenophylla*, to 3 m (10 ft), evergreen yellow flowers followed by berries

Trimming: trim deciduous kinds to shape in late winter, evergreen kinds in spring after flowers fade

Cultivation and uses: no special requirements. Good as both boundary and internal hedges

Box
Buxus

Site: full sun or partial shade, useful in seaside areas

Soil: light, well drained

Height: up to 3 m (10 ft)

Type of plant: hardy, slow-growing evergreen shrub

Planting time: spring or autumn

Planting distance: 45 cm (1½ ft) for *B. sempervirens*, 23 to 30 cm (9 to 12 in) for *B. s. suffruticosa*

Propagation: take cuttings of side shoots in late summer or early autumn. Divide *B. s. suffruticosa* in spring

Species cultivated: *B. sempervirens* and its many forms including variegated varieties such as 'Elegantissima' and 'Aureovariegata'. *B. s. suffruticosa* is the edging box, dwarf growing to 90 cm (3 ft)

Trimming: trim in summer; do any hard cutting back in spring. *B. s. suffruticosa* will need trimming two or three times in summer

Cultivation and uses: mulch occasionally with decayed manure or garden compost. The soil must be well dug and prepared before planting

Hornbeam

Carpinus betulus

Site: sun or shade, good for exposed positions

Soil: good, deep, clay or chalk

Height: 3 to 6 m (10 to 20 ft)

Type of plant: hardy deciduous tree

Planting time: autumn or late winter

Planting distance: 45 cm (18 in)

Propagation: sow seeds outdoors in autumn

Species cultivated: *C. betulus*; among its forms is *C. betulus* 'Variegata' with leaves marked with white

Trimming: do not prune for the first two years, then trim to required shape in late summer. Allow to reach the required height before taking the tops of the plants off

Cultivation and uses: similar to beech in appearance, old leaves retained in the hedge until spring. Mulch annually with leafmould, garden compost or decayed manure

False Cypress

Chamaecyparis

Site: open, away from other trees. Golden varieties grow best in full sun

Soil: any, good preparation before planting is essential

Height: fast growing, average height 3 to 4.5 m (10 to 15 ft)

Type of plant: hardy conifer

Planting time: autumn or spring

Planting distance: 60 to 90 cm (2 to 3 ft)

Propagation: take cuttings from midsummer to autumn

Species cultivated: *C. lawsoniana* and its many varieties which include *allumii* glaucous blue, *fletcheri*, blue grey, 'Green Hedger' rich green; 'Triomf van Boskoop' (photograph) glaucous blue

Trimming: trim in early summer and early autumn, do any hard pruning in mid spring. Allow to reach the required height before cutting the top

Cultivation and uses: no special requirements. Makes a good windscreen

Hawthorn, May

Crataegus

Site: sun or partial shade

Soil: ordinary

Height: 2 to 4.5 m (6 to 15 ft)

Type of plant: deciduous, thorny tree

Flowers: white, scented, followed in autumn by crimson haws

Flowering time: late spring, early summer

Planting time: spring or autumn

Planting distance: 30 to 38 cm (12 to 15 in)

Propagation: by seeds, first stratified for 18 months and then sown outdoors in late winter or spring

Species cultivated: *C. monogyna* (photograph) is the most usual, also *C. oxyacantha* and its varieties

Trimming: will withstand hard pruning if necessary. Trim several times from early to late summer

Cultivation and uses: no special requirements. Can withstand exposure and periods of drought once established

Leyland Cypress

× *Cupressocyparis*

Site: sunny or partly shaded, tolerant of a wide range of conditions

Soil: ordinary, well drained, fairly deep

Height: 1.25 to 3.5 m (4 to 11 ft)

Type of plant: hardy conifer, fast growing

Planting time: early autumn or spring

Planting distance: 60 to 90 cm (2 to 3 ft)

Propagation: take cuttings of young growth and root them in a propagator in summer

Species cultivated: × *C. leylandii* (photograph) and its various forms. There is an especially good golden form 'Castlewellan'

Trimming: trim in late summer. Allow plants to exceed the required height of the hedge by about 30 cm (1 ft) and then cut them back by about 45 cm (18 in)

Cultivation and uses: give an annual dressing of fertiliser. Also makes a good specimen tree

Beech

Fagus

Site: sun or partly shaded

Soil: sandy or chalky, good drainage is essential

Height: 1.25 to 3 m (4 to 10 ft)

Type of plant: hardy deciduous tree

Planting time: autumn or late winter

Planting distance: 45 cm (18 in)

Propagation: by seeds stratified and then sown outdoors or in a frame

Species cultivated: *F. sylvatica*, the common beech, and its many forms including the copper beech *F. s. purpurea*

Trimming: keep sides well trimmed, doing this in autumn or winter but do not trim for the first two years. Do not cut the leading shoots until the hedge has exceeded the required height

Cultivation and uses: no special requirements. The dead brown leaves are retained in the hedge all winter and provide good cover as well as making an efficient windbreak

Holly

Ilex

Site: from sun to full shade

Soil: any

Height: 1.25 to 3.5 m (4 to 11 ft)

Type of plant: hardy, slow-growing evergreen tree

Planting time: early autumn or spring

Planting distance: 45 to 60 cm (18 to 24 in)

Propagation: by seeds stratified for twelve months and then sown outdoors; variegated kinds by cuttings taken in summer and rooted in a propagator

Species cultivated: many varieties and forms of *I. aquifolium* (photograph) in green, gold and silver. Look for 'Golden King' yellow-edged leaves, 'Golden Queen' gold-edged leaves, 'Silver Queen' cream-edged leaves, 'Argenteo-marginata' silver-edged leaves

Trimming: trim in late summer but do any severe cutting back in spring. Few berries are produced when holly is grown as a hedge

Cultivation and uses: before planting, dig the ground well and incorporate some decayed manure or garden compost. Water well during dry periods until hedge is completely established

Privet
Ligustrum

Site: shaded to full sun

Soil: ordinary

Height: 60 cm to 3.5 m (2 to 11 ft)

Type of plant: hardy, fast-growing evergreen or semi-evergreen shrub

Planting time: autumn or spring

Planting distance: 30 to 45 cm (12 to 18 in)

Propagation: take hardwood cuttings in autumn

Species cultivated: for hedges, *L. ovalifolium* semi-evergreen and its golden form 'Aureum' (photograph) are good choices. *L. vulgare*, common privet, semi-evergreen can also be used

Trimming: trim as necessary in spring and summer

Cultivation and uses: very tolerant of poor conditions. After planting cut back to within 30 cm (12 in) of ground level. Makes a good dense boundary hedge

Firethorn
Pyracantha

Site: light shade and full sun

Soil: ordinary, well drained

Height: to 4.5 m (15 ft) depending on species

Type of plant: hardy evergreen shrub with spiny branches and white flowers in late spring

Planting time: spring or autumn

Planting distance: 45 to 60 cm (18 to 24 in) apart

Propagation: by seeds sown in spring; take half-ripe cuttings in summer or early autumn

Species cultivated: *P. lalandei*, orange-red berries, up to 2.5 m (8 ft); *P. rogersiana*, reddish-orange berries, to 2 m (6 ft); *P. watereri* (illustrated) red berries, to 2 m (6 ft)

Trimming: trim in spring preferably using secateurs. Clipped hedges will not carry many berries

Cultivation and uses: very good screening plants, ideal for towns and industrial areas. No special requirements

Yew
Taxus

Site: shaded to full sun, very tolerant

Soil: well drained, good

Height: 1.25 to 4.5 m (4 to 15 ft)

Type of plant: hardy conifer, all parts are poisonous except the red flesh of the fruits

Planting time: early autumn or spring

Planting distance: 45 to 60 cm (1½ to 2 ft)

Propagation: take cuttings of young growth and insert in a propagator in summer or in a frame in autumn; also by hardwood cuttings in autumn

Species cultivated: the common yew, *T. baccata* and its golden form *aurea* are the best for clipping and topiary work (photograph)

Trimming: leave for a year before clipping and then trim in midsummer. Clip so that the hedge tapers towards the top

Cultivation and uses: plant small plants to get the best hedge; prepare the ground well by working in decayed compost or manure. Water well if conditions are dry after planting and spray the leaves with water until the plants are established

Arbor-Vitae
Thuja

Site: sun or partly shaded

Soil: ordinary and deep, well drained

Height: 1.25 to 3.5 m (4 to 11 ft)

Type of plant: hardy conifer

Planting time: autumn or spring

Planting distance: 60 to 90 cm (2 to 3 ft)

Propagation: take cuttings of young growth and insert in a propagator in summer or take cuttings of older growth and root in a frame in autumn

Species cultivated: *T. occidentalis*, the American arbor-vitae, and its varieties such as 'Pyramidalis compacta' (photograph). Also *T. plicata* and its many varieties

Trimming: trim in late summer from the second growing season. Allow to reach the required height before cutting the top.

Cultivation and uses: keep well watered after planting if dry weather occurs and spray the foliage with water

Herbaceous Perennials

The time has long passed when herbaceous perennials were looked on solely as plants to grow in long, formal borders. Nowadays, it is possible to see them used in the most imaginative way in gardens everywhere – in island beds in lawn settings; in mixed borders which include selected shrubs, bulbous plants, annuals and perhaps even a small tree; and as set-piece plantings in key positions in the garden. They can be used in so many different ways to create special effects between spring and autumn.

Certainly island beds which you can view from every angle allow you to do exciting things, whether the intention is to have a spread of colour over a long season or to create a dramatic display over a relatively short period. In the smaller garden it is probably better to go for the first option.

What you must always try to do with herbaceous perennials which are grouped to give a long period of interest is to position them in such a way that not only are they in harmony one with the other but they are planned to give their display so that there are no large areas at any one time which lack interest. The best way to achieve this is to sit down with a sheet of paper and a pencil and work out a planting plan. A good job for a wet winter weekend!

When planning a bed or border there is much which can be done to exploit the different colouring, forms and heights of perennial plants. Contrast the architectural outline of *Acanthus spinosus* with the charm of the massed spikes of that very popular salvia *S.* × *superba*, or the sword-like foliage and lily-like flowers of the hemerocallises, the day lilies, with the incredible floral profusion of the daisy-flowered *Coreopsis verticillata*. With perennials you have the opportunity to experiment to your heart's content.

One thing always to keep in mind is the advisability of making bold groups of each plant; individual specimens will not make an impact. Of course, in the main, one wants the tall plants in the rear, the medium-sized plants in the middle and the low-growing kinds in the front in a conventional border (it is different with an island bed) but don't be too rigid about this for the way the heights of the plants are varied can be almost as important as the colour blending.

Preparation for planting

Ideally, get the ground ready for perennials as early in winter as possible, especially if the soil is heavy. Nothing breaks down clay soils more effectively than exposure to frost and rain after it has been dug and left in rough lumps.

The planting season which is most satisfactory for the vast majority of perennials is undoubtedly early to mid-spring, although it is perfectly satisfactory to start in late winter in those years when the weather is not severe at that time. In frost-free climates winter is the best time. However, plants which take their time about settling down (peonies and hellebores are examples) are probably best started off in the early part of autumn. Before planting, remove as many of the perennial weeds as possible – things such as couch grass and the perennial nettle if left will quickly spread and be impossible to eradicate.

Planting

In all cases plant firmly, working the soil well in among the roots. Use a trowel to make the holes large enough to accommodate the roots or root balls. For best effect it is advisable to plant in groups of a kind placing three, five, seven or more of each variety together.

Care and feeding

Many perennials need no support, but almost all those which do, with the exception of lupins and delphiniums which need proper stakes, are perfectly well served by pea sticks or twiggy branches of such a height that they will be completely hidden when the plants have grown up through them.

One of the most important chores with perennials is to fork over the soil in between the plants before growth starts in spring and at the same time work into the surface soil a light dressing of slow-acting bonemeal. Quick-acting fertilisers will just encourage the plants to make excess growth at the expense of flowering. The production of more flowers is also likely to be encouraged if you go round removing spent blooms.

Dividing

Generally speaking, perennials need lifting and dividing every third or fourth year in autumn or spring (preferably the spring for all but the slow establishers). When division is necessary there will be signs of deterioration in the quality of the plants and their blooms. Large clumps can best be divided by driving two forks into them back to back and prising them apart, but many plants can be divided just by pulling the root clumps apart. It is the outside portions which are retained and the old, worn-out inner parts which are discarded. The divisions must, of course, have healthy roots and at least one shoot.

Naturally, at such a time you will take the opportunity to improve the soil before replanting, digging in humus-forming material like garden compost or peat to improve the structure.

Growing from seed

You can also grow perennials from seed, if you are prepared to wait for the resulting plants to reach flowering size. A lot of popular perennials are listed by seedsmen from delphiniums to lupins, primulas and rudbeckias, but, with exceptions like *Geum* 'Mrs Bradshaw' and *Rudbeckia* 'Goldsturm', varieties do not come true from seed. Strains are a different matter for with these the desired qualities of colour, habit and free-flowering are carried through with very little variation indeed.

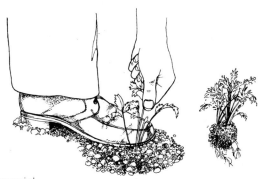

Planting a perennial

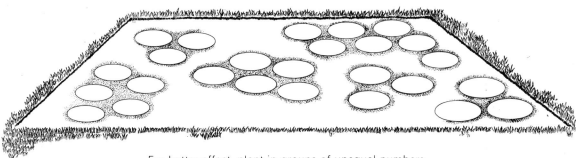

For better effect, plant in groups of unequal numbers

When planting a border, the plants are
graded in size towards the back

When planting an island bed, the
tallest plants are in the middle

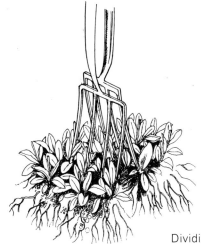
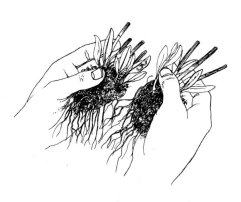

Dividing old root clumps

Bear's Breeches
Acanthus

Site: sunny, or partly shaded, sheltered

Soil: well drained, sandy

Height: up to 120 cm (4 ft)

Spread: up to 90 cm (3 ft)

Flowers: white, lilac, purple

Flowering time: summer

When to sow: spring

Planting time: mid autumn or spring is best – protect during the first winter

Propagation: take root cuttings in winter; sow seeds in light soil; divide in spring or autumn

Species cultivated: *A. mollis* (photograph), white and purple flowers, broadly lobed leaves and its hardier form *latifolius*; *A. spinosus*, purple flowers, deeply lobed spiny leaves

Cultivation and uses: very ornamental foliage and best planted in front of a border. Flower spikes can be used in dried flower arrangements. Cut stems back to ground level after flowering. Lift and divide only when overcrowded

Yarrow
Achillea

Site: sunny

Soil: well drained, ordinary

Height: up to 120 cm (4 ft)

Spread: up to 60 cm (2 ft)

Flowers: yellow, white, pink

Flowering time: mid to late summer

When to sow: early spring

Planting time: mid autumn; mid to late spring is best

Propagation: sow seeds under glass; divide roots in autumn or spring

Species cultivated: many species and garden varieties available including *A. filipendulina*, yellow flowers, 120 cm (4 ft) and its varieties such as 'Gold Plate' and 'Parker's Variety' (photograph); *A. millefolium* 'Fire King', deep red flowers, 1 m (3 ft); *A. ptarmica*, white flowers, 60 cm (2 ft). Also dwarf species suitable for a rockery such as *A. tomentosa*, sulphur-yellow flowers, 15 to 20 cm (6 to 8 in)

Cultivation and uses: good border and rock garden plants; can be used for cut flowers, dry well. Cut back to ground level in late autumn

Monkshood

Aconitum

Site: light shade or sun

Soil: moist, ordinary

Height: up to 1.5 m (5 ft) needs staking

Spread: up to 60 cm (2 ft)

Flowers: blue, purple, pink, yellow, sometimes with white

Flowering time: summer to early autumn

When to sow: mid spring

Planting time: spring, but best in autumn

Propagation: divide roots in autumn or spring; sow seeds in open ground

Species cultivated: among the many kinds are *A. napellus* 'Carneum' pink flowers, *A. lycoctonum* up to 1.5 m (5 ft), yellow flowers, 'Bressingham Spire' violet blue, 90 cm (3 ft) 'Spark's Variety' dark blue, 1.5 m (5 ft)

Cultivation and uses: flowers can be cut but the roots are poisonous, attractive foliage. Needs thinning and replanting every few years, cut down flowering stems in autumn

African Lily

Agapanthus

Site: sunny, warm. In cool climates may be more reliable as a greenhouse plant

Soil: deep, well drained

Height: up to 90 cm (3 ft)

Spread: up to 45 cm (1½ ft)

Flowers: white, blue, violet

Flowering time: summer

When to sow: mid spring

Planting time: mid spring, position the crowns about 5 cm (2 in) below ground level

Propagation: divide roots in early spring; sow seeds in spring in 13 to 15°C (55 to 59°F)

Species cultivated: *A. africanus* (photograph) up to 1 m (3 ft), blue flowers in late summer, evergreen strap-shaped foliage, there is a white variety 'Albus'; *A. campanulatus* up to 60 cm (2 ft), deep blue flowers in late summer; *A. caulescens* up to 120 cm (4 ft), lilac-blue flowers in late summer, deciduous. The deciduous species are slightly hardier than the evergreen species

Cultivation and uses: good plants for growing in tubs when they can be moved into a greenhouse in winter. Outdoors, protect the roots from frost with a layer of straw or bracken

Lady's Mantle
Alchemilla

Site: sunny, light shade

Soil: well drained, ordinary

Height: up to 45 cm (1½ ft)

Spread: up to 38 cm (15 in)

Flowers: yellow, green

Flowering time: summer

When to sow: spring

Planting time: spring or autumn

Propagation: sow seeds in a frame or outdoors; divide roots in spring or autumn

Species cultivated: *A. mollis* (photograph), up to 45 cm (1½ ft), delicate greeny yellow flowers produced throughout summer; *A. alpina*, up to 15 cm (6 in), silvery foliage, greeny flowers throughout summer

Cultivation and uses: front of a border, between paving slabs and as ground cover. After flowering cut down stems to 2.5 cm (1 in) above ground

Peruvian Lily
Alstroemeria

Site: sunny, sheltered

Soil: well drained, deep, fertile

Height: up to 90 cm (3 ft)

Spread: up to 45 cm (1½ ft)

Flowers: orange, pink, apricot, flame, lilac, white

Flowering time: midsummer

When to sow: spring

Planting time: spring, cover roots with 15 cm (6 in) of soil

Propagation: sow seeds in 15 to 18°C (59 to 64°F); divide clumps in spring, separate each individual plant and pot up. Replant the following spring

Species cultivated: *A. aurantiaca* (photograph) 90 cm (3 ft), orange, two upper petals marked with red and yellow; a number of named varieties are available. *A. ligtu*, 60 cm (2 ft), is found in shades of pink or purple, it has a number of hybrids of various colours

Cultivation and uses: long-lasting cut flowers. Remove dead flowers and cut stems back to ground level when foliage dies. In cold areas, protect from frost with a layer of straw or bracken

Pearl Everlasting
Anaphalis

Site: sunny

Soil: well drained, ordinary, not too dry

Height: up to 60 cm (2 ft)

Spread: up to 38 cm (15 in)

Flowers: white with yellow eyes

Flowering time: summer

When to sow: spring

Planting time: mid autumn to early spring

Propagation: sow seeds in pots; divide clumps in spring or autumn

Species cultivated: *A. margaritacea* (photograph) 45 to 60 cm (1½ to 2 ft), white flowers and grey foliage; *A. triplinervis*, white, downy grey leaves, 30 to 45 cm (1 to 1½ ft)

Cultivation and uses: the everlasting flowers can be dried and used in flower arrangements. If plants get untidy, cut them hard back in autumn

Alkanet
Anchusa

Site: sunny

Soil: fertile, well drained

Height: up to 1.5 m (5 ft)

Spread: up to 60 cm (2 ft)

Flowers: blue

Flowering time: late spring to midsummer

When to sow: mid spring

When to plant: mid autumn to early spring

Propagation: sow seeds outdoors; take root cuttings in winter or, in the case of *A. caespitosa*, in the spring; *A. angustissima* should be divided in the spring

Species cultivated: *A. angustissima*, 30 cm (1 ft) has tough hairy stems; *A. azurea* (syn. *italica*) (photograph) is much taller and has a number of named varieties in all shades of blue; *A. caespitosa* is a rock garden plant 8 cm (3 in) high

Cultivation and uses: taller varieties as border or island bed plants, lower growing species are suitable for the rock garden. Cut down old stems in autumn. Support with twigs or canes if necessary

Chamomile
Anthemis

Site: sunny

Soil: well drained, ordinary

Height: up to 90 cm (3 ft)

Spread: up to 90 cm (3 ft)

Flowers: yellow

Flowering time: early to midsummer

When to sow: mid spring

Planting time: early spring or autumn

Propagation: sow seeds outdoors; divide plants in early spring or autumn; take softwood cuttings in spring

Species cultivated: these include *A. nobilis* white flowers, 30 cm (1 ft), fragrant leaves, flowers used to make tea; *A. sancti-johannis*, orange-yellow flowers, up to 90 cm (3 ft); *A. tinctoria* (photograph), 60 to 90 cm (2 to 3 ft), yellow and its hybrids such as 'E. C. Buxton' pale yellow and 'Grallagh Gold' deep yellow

Cultivation and uses: all have strongly scented foliage and make good border plants. *A. nobilis* can be used for a lawn. Cut down old flower stems, divide and replant in spring if affected by frost and snow

Columbine
Aquilegia

Site: partial shade or sunny

Soil: moist but well drained

Height: up to 90 cm (3 ft)

Spread: up to 45 cm (1½ ft)

Flowers: white, yellow, crimson, pink, blue, violet, often attractively combined

Flowering time: early summer

When to sow: spring

Planting time: mid spring or autumn

Propagation: divide roots in mid spring; sow seeds in a frame or out of doors

Species cultivated: these include *A. alpina*, pale blue, late spring, 30 cm (1 ft); *A. bertolonii*, deep blue, late spring and early summer, 15 cm (6 in); *A. vulgaris*, blue, purple or white, single or double flowers up to 60 cm (2 ft). There are also many hybrids (photograph), good mixed strains are Mrs Scott Elliott Hybrids and McKana Giant Hybrids

Cultivation and uses: not long lived, cut stems to ground level in autumn. Delicate, graceful flowers for the border or rock garden

Michaelmas Daisy
Aster

Site: sunny, open or lightly shaded

Soil: moist, so it will not dry out in late summer

Height: 15 cm (6 in) to 120 cm (4 ft)

Spread: depends on variety

Flowers: blue, violet, red, purple, white, pink, single or double

Flowering time: autumn

When to sow: spring

Planting time: spring or autumn

Propagation: divide roots in autumn or spring – the latter time best; sow seeds out of doors or under glass; take softwood cuttings in spring

Species cultivated: there are many good garden varieties which vary greatly both in size of plant and flower. The varieties of *A. novi-belgii* are among the most popular (photograph)

Cultivation and uses: the dwarf forms, 15 cm (6 in), are good in the front of the border; all kinds provide colour late in the year. Divide and thin clumps every few years. Cut down stems from late autumn

False Goat's Beard
Astilbe

Site: light shade, sunny

Soil: moist, plenty of water required in dry weather

Height: up to 2 m (6 ft)

Spread: up to 90 cm (3 ft)

Flowers: white, pink, red

Flowering time: summer

Planting time: spring or autumn

Propagation: divide roots in spring or autumn

Species cultivated: *A. arendsii*, white to red, 60 cm to 1.5 m (2 to 5 ft); *A. chinensis* and varieties, white, purple and pink, late summer, 15 to 60 cm (6 in to 2 ft); *A. davidii*, magenta flowers, late summer, 1.2 to 2 m (4 to 6 ft). There are other species and a large range of garden varieties (photograph) which vary in height and flower colour

Cultivation and uses: good poolside planting, dead flowers decorative in winter. Water well in dry weather and mulch with peat or leafmould. Cut stems back in spring; lift and divide every 3 years

Elephant's Ears, Megasea
Bergenia

Site: partial shade or sunny

Soil: good, rather moist

Height: 38 cm (15 in)

Spread: 60 cm (2 ft)

Flowers: rose pink, white

Flowering time: early spring

Planting time: spring or autumn

Propagation: divide roots in spring or autumn

Species cultivated: *B. cordifolia*, pink flowers, 38 cm (15 in); *B. crassifolia*, rose purple, 45 cm (1½ ft); *B. × schmidtii* (photograph), pink 30 cm (1 ft); *B. stracheyi*, pinkish white, 23 to 30 cm (9 to 12 in) and its variety 'Silver Light'

Uses: good ground cover for borders or woods, foliage almost evergreen. Cut off faded flowers; lift and divide only when overcrowded

Knapweed, Cornflower
Centaurea

Site: sunny, warm, sheltered

Soil: ordinary, well drained

Height: up to 1.5 m (5 ft)

Spread: up to 60 cm (2 ft)

Flowers: yellow, pink, blue, white

Flowering time: late spring to late summer

When to sow: spring

Planting time: spring or autumn

Propagation: divide in spring or autumn; sow seeds in 15 to 18°C (59 to 64°F)

Species cultivated: *C. montana*, blue flowers late spring to early summer, 60 cm (2 ft) tall; *C. dealbata*, rose flowers, summer, up to 90 cm (3 ft) tall; *C. macrocephala* (photograph), yellow flowers in summer, 90 cm (3 ft). There are a number of tender species with silvery foliage such as *C. gymnocarpa* and *rutifolia* which may not survive the winter outdoors in cooler climates

Uses: good cut flowers; can be dried; suitable for warm dry places. Cut off dead flowers; lift and divide every 3 years or so

Valerian

Centranthus

Site: sunny

Soil: well drained, ordinary, stony

Height: up to 75 cm (2½ ft)

Spread: up to 45 cm (1½ ft)

Flowers: red, pink or white

Flowering time: summer

When to sow: spring

Planting time: spring or autumn

Propagation: sow seeds in light soil; divide in spring or autumn

Species cultivated: *C. ruber* (photograph), rose-red 45 cm (18 in) and its varieties 'Albus' white and 'Coccineus' crimson

Cultivation and uses: grows well in hot, dry conditions on banks and in walls. Cut away any dead stems from late autumn

Shasta Daisy

Chrysanthemum

Site: sunny, open

Soil: ordinary

Height: up to 90 cm (3 ft)

Spread: up to 45 cm (18 in)

Flowers: white, single or double

Flowering time: summer

When to sow: spring, early summer

Planting time: spring or autumn

Propagation: divide roots in autumn or spring; sow seed outdoors or in a frame

Species cultivated: *C. maximum* and its varieties (photograph) such as 'Bishopstone', 'Cobham Gold' double with a yellow centre, and 'Esther Read'. Some have fringed petals

Cultivation and uses: excellent border plant, good cut flowers. Cut stems back to ground level in winter, lift and divide every 3 years or so

Tickseed
Coreopsis

Site: sunny

Soil: well drained, ordinary

Height: up to 120 cm (4 ft)

Spread: bushy habit, 45 cm (1½ ft)

Flowers: yellow, some marked with red

Flowering time: midsummer to early autumn

When to sow: spring or early summer

Planting time: spring

Propagation: by careful division in spring; sow seeds outdoors in spring or early summer, transplant seedlings to permanent position when big enough to handle

Species cultivated: *C. grandiflora*, yellow, 60 to 90 cm (2 to 3 ft); *C. auriculata*, yellow and red, 60 to 90 cm (2 to 3 ft); *C. verticillata* (photograph), yellow, 60 cm (2 ft)

Uses: good cut flowers; colourful plants for the border. Provide support for the taller varieties; cut off dead flowers; lift and divide when overcrowded

Pampas Grass
Cortaderia

Site: sunny, warm, sheltered

Soil: deep, well drained

Height: up to 3 m (10 ft)

Spread: up to 2.5 m (8 ft)

Flowers: creamy white plumes

Flowering time: late summer to late autumn

Sowing time: spring

Planting time: late spring

Propagation: divide in spring, do not let the roots get dry; sow seeds in spring in 15 to 18°C (59 to 64°F)

Species cultivated: *C. selloana* (photograph), up to 3 m (10 ft), silvery plumes, those from female plants being silkier and more durable; *C. s. carnea* has plumes tinged pink; *C. s. pumila* is more compact, 1.5 m (5 ft)

Cultivation and uses: lovely specimen plants; the flower heads (plumes) are useful for dried flower arrangements – gather as soon as fully developed. Remove dead leaves in spring (wear gloves for this operation as the leaf edges are sharp)

Delphinium
Delphinium

Site: sunny, sheltered

Soil: deep, well drained, fertile

Height: up to 2.5 m (8 ft)

Spread: up to 60 cm (2 ft)

Flowers: white, cream, violet, blue, orange, scarlet, purple, double and single

Flowering time: summer

Sowing time: early autumn, as soon as ripe

Planting time: autumn or spring

Propagation: take softwood cuttings in spring; divide in spring; sow seeds where plants are to flower

Species cultivated: most garden varieties are hybrids bred from *D. elatum* and *D. grandiflorum*. There are two main groups, large flowered or Elatum hybrids (photograph) up to 2.5 m (8 ft) and the flowers may be single, semi-double or double. The Belladonna varieties are up to 1.5 m (5 ft) tall and are more graceful

Cultivation and uses: good for the back of a border; cut off faded flowers to get a second crop; cut stems back to ground level in autumn; support taller kinds with canes

Bleeding Heart
Dicentra

Site: light shade or sun, sheltered

Soil: well drained, deep, fertile

Height: up to 120 cm (4 ft)

Spread: up to 45 cm (1½ ft)

Flowers: red, pink, white

Flowering time: late spring to summer

When to sow: spring

When to plant: mid autumn or early spring

Propagation: sow seeds outdoors; divide plants in mid autumn or early spring; take root cuttings in early spring

Species cultivated: *D. spectabilis* (photograph), red heart-shaped flowers; *D. formosa* pink flowers; *D. eximia* narrow pink flowers, and variety 'Alba' with white flowers. All have attractive fern-like foliage

Uses: a graceful plant for the border; can be grown as a pot plant. Once established do not disturb. Remove dead flower stems

Leopard's Bane
Doronicum

Site: sunny or lightly shaded

Soil: deep, moist

Height: up to 90 cm (3 ft)

Spread: up to 60 cm (2 ft)

Flowers: yellow

Flowering time: spring

Sowing time: spring

Planting time: autumn or spring

Propagation: divide the roots in autumn or spring; sow seeds outdoors in spring or early summer

Species cultivated: *D. austriacum*, yellow flowers and bright green foliage, 45 cm (18 in); *D. caucasicum* 30 to 45 cm (1 to 1½ ft); *D. plantagineum* 'Harpur Crewe' an improved form of the species, 75 to 90 cm (2½ to 3 ft). *D. cordatum* is a small species, 15 cm (6 in) high

Cultivation and uses: good cut flowers. Remove dead flowers regularly; cut stems down in autumn

Globe Thistle
Echinops

Site: sunny, open

Soil: ordinary, well drained

Height: up to 1.5 m (5 ft)

Spread: up to 60 cm (2 ft)

Flowers: metallic blue or white

Flowering time: midsummer to early autumn

When to sow: spring

Planting time: spring or autumn

Propagation: sow seeds outdoors; divide roots in spring; take root cuttings in winter

Species cultivated: *E. ritro* (photograph), blue flowers, grey-green foliage, 90 cm (3 ft); *E. nivalis*, white flowers, grey foliage, 2 m (6 ft). Two recommended varieties are 'Blue Globe' and 'Taplow Blue'

Uses: these thistle-like plants are useful in flower arrangements, they can also be dried. Cut the stems back to ground level in autumn

Barrenwort

Epimedium

Site: partial shade

Soil: moist

Height: up to 30 cm (1 ft)

Spread: up to 30 cm (1 ft)

Flowers: white, cream, yellow, pink, purple

Flowering time: late spring

Planting time: autumn or spring

Propagation: divide the roots in autumn

Species cultivated: *E.* × *rubrum* (photograph), 23 cm (9 in), small star-shaped crimson and yellow flowers in sprays produced in spring; *E.* × *versicolor*, 30 cm (1 ft), rose and yellow coloured flowers in spring, leaves tint in spring and autumn; *E.* × *youngianum*, 23 cm (9 in), greenish white flowers in spring

Cultivation and uses: grown mainly for foliage; good ground cover as they creep by rhizomes, suitable for planting under trees, woodland garden. Cut off old leaves or stems in late winter. Mulch with peat or leafmould in spring

Foxtail Lily

Eremurus

Site: sunny, warm

Soil: deep, well drained, sandy, well manured

Height: up to 2.5 m (8 ft)

Spread: up to 90 cm (3 ft)

Flowers: yellow, white, orange or pink

Flowering time: early to midsummer

Sowing time: spring

Planting time: autumn or spring – autumn is best

Propagation: divide in autumn or spring; sow seeds in heat, keep in cold frame for three years, seeds are often slow to germinate.

Species cultivated: *E. robustus*, pink or white flowers, late spring or early summer, 2.5 m (8 ft); *E. stenophyllus* (photograph), yellow flowers in early summer, to 120 cm (4 ft). Many good hybrids including the 'Highdown' varieties in a range of colours

Cultivation and uses: as cut flowers, striking border plants. Roots resent disturbance; mulch with well decayed manure in autumn; protect in winter with dried bracken; water in hot weather. Some need staking.

Fleabane, Erigeron

Erigeron

Site: sunny, open

Soil: well drained – especially for the orange kinds

Height: up to 60 cm (2 ft)

Spread: up to 60 cm (2 ft)

Flowers: white, cream, pink, violet, purple, blue

Flowering time: early to late summer

Sowing time: spring or early summer

Planting time: spring or autumn

Propagation: divide roots in spring or autumn, sow seeds outdoors

Species cultivated: *E. aureus*, golden flowers, early summer, 10 cm (4 in); *E. glaucus*, lavender or pink flowers, early summer, 23 cm (9 in); *E. macranthus*, violet-blue flowers, summer, 30 cm (1 ft). There are also many varieties (photograph) and these have larger flowers

Cultivation and uses: good for cutting; excellent border plants, grow well in seaside areas. Cut down stems after flowering and remove flowers as they fade. Larger kinds may need supporting

Sea Holly

Eryngium

Site: sunny

Soil: light, sandy, well drained, will thrive in poor soil

Height: up to 2 m (6 ft)

Spread: up to 60 cm (2 ft)

Flowers: white, green, purple, silvery blue

Flowering time: midsummer to early autumn

Sowing time: spring

Planting time: spring or autumn

Propagation: take root cuttings in winter and place in a frame or cool greenhouse; divide plants in spring; sow seeds in sandy soil in a frame

Species cultivated: *E. planum* (photograph), up to 90 cm (3 ft), blue flowers in summer; *E. alpinum*, up to 90 cm (3 ft), blue flowers in summer; *E. maritimum* up to 30 cm (1 ft), metallic blue flowers in summer, silvery foliage, much branched; *E. tripartitum*, up to 75 cm (2½ ft), silver-blue flowers, midsummer to early autumn

Uses: good for dried flower arrangements, very decorative foliage. May not survive in moist soils. Cut stems back to ground level in autumn

Spurge, Milkweed

Euphorbia

Site: light shade or sunny

Soil: fertile, fairly well drained

Height: up to 120 cm (4 ft)

Spread: up to 1 m (3 ft)

Flowers: insignificant, but surrounded by yellow or green bracts

Flowering time: spring to summer

Sowing time: spring or early summer, or as soon as ripe

Planting time: spring or autumn

Propagation: sow seeds outdoors; divide roots in spring or autumn; take cuttings immediately after flowering

Species cultivated: *E. polychroma* (syn. *epithymoides*) (photograph), up to 45 cm (1½ ft), lemon yellow bracts in spring; *E. characias*, up to 120 cm (4 ft), green bracts in early summer, evergreen in mild winters; *E. griffithii*, up to 90 cm (3 ft), brick red bracts in early summer, it has a good form called 'Fireglow'

Cultivation and uses: as cut flowers; interesting foliage, some species can be used as ground cover. Older plants resent disturbance.

Fescue Grass

Festuca

Site: sunny

Soil: ordinary

Height: up to 30 cm (12 in)

Spread: 15 cm (6 in)

Foliage colour: blue-green

Sowing time: spring

Planting time: autumn or spring

Propagation: sow seeds out of doors; divide clumps between autumn and spring

Species cultivated: *F. glauca* (photograph), bears spikes of purple flowers in summer and forms a tight clump; *F. amethystina* has more spreading leaves and darker flowers

Cultivation and uses: grown for its foliage; use as an edging plant. Cut off the dead flowers before the seeds are shed

Blanket Flower

Gaillardia

Site: sunny

Soil: well drained

Height: up to 60 cm (2 ft)

Spread: up to 45 cm (18 in)

Flowers: yellow, red, orange

Flowering time: midsummer to early autumn

Sowing time: spring

Planting time: late spring

Propagation: take cuttings in early spring; divide plants in spring; sow seeds at 15 to 18°C (59 to 64°F), plant out seedlings in late spring or early summer

Species cultivated: *G. aristata* has yellow outer florets around a red disc, the form 'Wirral Flame' is crimson with yellow-tipped petals; *G. pulchella* has double-flowered varieties. There are many good hybrids (photograph)

Cultivation and uses: suitable for cutting. Plants not usually long lived, usually need support. Cut off dead flowers

Cranesbill

Geranium

Site: light shade or sun

Soil: well drained, many grow well on chalk

Height: up to 60 cm (2 ft)

Spread: up to 60 cm (2 ft)

Flowers: blue, purple, pink, magenta or white

Flowering time: early to late summer

Sowing time: spring or early summer

Planting time: spring or autumn

Propagation: divide in spring or autumn; sow seeds outside in a sunny place or in a frame or greenhouse

Species cultivated: *G. endressii*, pink, summer, 30 cm (1 ft) tall; *G. grandiflorum*, blue, summer, 45 to 60 cm (1½ to 2 ft); 'Johnson's Blue' (photograph), lavender blue, early summer, 45 cm (1½ ft); *G. sanguineum lancastriense*, pink, summer, mat forming; *G. subcaulescens*, rosy-pink, spring to autumn, 15 to 23 cm (6 to 9 in)

Cultivation and uses: can be used as a ground cover plant and smaller kinds, such as *G. subcaulescens*, on the rock garden. Cut faded flower stems back to ground level to encourage fresh growth and more flowers. Lift and divide when overgrown

Avens

Geum

Site: sunny, warm, light shade

Soil: well drained, ordinary

Height: up to 60 cm (2 ft)

Spread: up to 30 cm (1 ft)

Flowers: yellow, orange, red

Flowering time: mid to late summer

Sowing time: spring

Planting time: spring or autumn

Propagation: divide in spring; sow seeds in a frame in spring or outdoors in late spring or early summer

Species cultivated: typical hybrids are 'Mrs Bradshaw' semi-double flowers, 60 cm (2 ft); 'Lady Strathedon' yellow, 60 cm (2 ft); 'Fire Opal' coppery.orange, 60 cm (2 ft); *G. borisii* is smaller – 30 cm (1 ft) – with orange-red flowers

Cultivation and uses: as cut flowers; colourful border plants. Cut down flower stems in autumn, divide every few years

Sneezeweed

Helenium

Site: sunny, open

Soil: well drained, ordinary

Height: up to 1.5 m (5 ft)

Spread: up to 50 cm (20 in)

Flowers: yellow, red, brown, orange

Flowering time: summer to early autumn

Sowing time: spring

Planting time: spring or autumn, spring is best

Propagation: divide in spring or autumn; sow seeds outdoors in spring

Species cultivated: *H. autumnale*, up to 1.5 m (5 ft), yellow and brown flowers in early autumn, is a parent of many garden hybrids (photograph); 'Moerheim Beauty' up to 1 m (3 ft), bronzy red flowers midsummer to early autumn; 'Golden Youth' up to 75 cm (2½ ft), yellow flowers, early to midsummer; 'Mahogany' up to 75 cm (2½ ft), yellow and red flowers, mid to late summer

Cultivation and uses: good as cut flowers; free flowering plants. Support stems if necessary; remove faded flowers and cut down the stems in autumn; lift and divide every 3 years

Sunflower

Helianthus

Site: sunny

Soil: good, well drained

Height: up to 2 m (7 ft)

Spread: up to 50 cm (20 in)

Flowers: yellow

Flowering time: late summer to mid autumn

Planting time: spring or autumn

Propagation: divide in spring or autumn; sow seeds
outdoors in spring or early summer

Species cultivated: *H. decapetalus*, up to 2 m (6 ft),
sulphur-yellow flowers, late summer, early autumn;
H. × multiflorus (photograph) golden yellow. Good
varieties include 'Loddon Gold' double golden yellow,
1.5 m (5 ft); 'Monarch' yellow, up to 2.25 m (7 ft)

Cultivation and uses: cut down flower stems in autumn,
lift and replant every second or third year. Good border
plants

Hellebore, Christmas Rose

Helleborus

Site: light shade

Soil: moist, well drained and fertile

Height: up to 60 cm (2 ft)

Spread: up to 45 cm (1½ ft)

Flower colour: white, green, maroon

Flowering time: winter, mid to late spring

When to sow: spring

Planting time: spring or autumn

Propagation: sow seeds in a frame; divide the roots in
spring (divide *H. atrorubens* in early autumn)

Species cultivated: *H. niger* (Christmas rose)
(photograph) white flowers appear in winter; *H.
orientalis* (Lenten rose) has white to pink to maroon
flowers appearing in spring; *H. atrorubens* has deep maroon
flowers which open from mid winter to spring;
H. foetidus (stinking hellebore) greenish flowers which
open in spring, this variety is evergreen; *H. viridis*
(green hellebore) has green flowers which open from
late winter to early spring

Cultivation and uses: these give winter interest to the
garden; can be used as cut flowers. Resent disturbance
once planted so do not divide unless essential

Day Lily

Hemerocallis

Site: light shade or sunny

Soil: deep reasonably fertile, not too dry

Height: up to 1 m (3 ft)

Spread: up to 1 m (3 ft)

Flowers: yellow, orange, pink

Flowering time: late spring to late summer

Sowing time: spring

Planting time: autumn or early spring

Propagation: divide in spring or autumn; sow seeds in 15 to 18°C (59 to 64°F); remove offshoots from flower stems in summer and root in frame or propagator

Species cultivated: many species include *H. citrina*, lemon-yellow flowers with a faint perfume, late summer, 90 cm (3 ft); *H. flava*, yellow, spring, 45 cm (2½ ft). Also a wide range of good hybrids (photograph)

Cultivation and uses: good ground cover; replant every 3 or 4 years, remove faded flowers regularly, mulch with decayed manure or garden compost in spring

Plantain Lily, Funkia

Hosta

Site: sunny or shady, susceptible to spring frosts

Soil: moist, with added leafmould or garden compost

Height: up to 60 cm (2 ft)

Spread: up to 60 cm (2 ft)

Flowers: white, cream, violet

Flowering time: summer

Planting time: spring or autumn

Propagation: divide in spring

Species cultivated: *H. sieboldiana elegans* (photograph), up to 60 cm (2 ft), pale violet flowers in summer; *H. crispula*, up to 75 cm (2½ ft), large broad dark green leaves edged with white, lilac flowers in early summer; *H. fortunei*, up to 75 cm (2½ ft), large leaves green above, bluish-white below, wavy edged, lilac flowers in summer; *H. undulata*, up to 45 cm (1½ ft), wavy leaves pale green with a white middle streak, lilac flowers late summer

Cultivation and uses: striking foliage, larger leaves when grown in shade but more flowers in a sunny position, makes good ground cover beside water. Topdress annually with decayed manure or garden compost

Incarvillea

Incarvillea

Site: sunny, sheltered

Soil: rich, well drained

Height: up to 60 cm (2 ft)

Spread: up to 30 cm (1 ft)

Flowers: rose, trumpet shaped

Flowering time: late spring to early summer

Sowing time: spring

Planting time: spring

Propagation: divide in spring; sow seeds in 15 to 18°C (59 to 64°F), seedlings grow slowly and may take several years to reach flowering size

Species cultivated: *I. delarayi* (photograph), rose red flowers in early summer, 60 cm (2 ft); *I. mairei*, rose red and yellow flowers, late spring, early summer, 30 cm (1 ft) tall

Cultivation and uses: effective in borders and island beds. In cold places protect crowns (centres) of the plants in winter with a covering of dry straw or bracken

Bearded Iris

Iris

Site: sunny

Soil: well drained, limy

Height: up to 1 m (3 ft)

Spread: up to 30 cm (1 ft)

Flowers: all colours

Flowering time: late spring to early summer

Planting time: spring, summer – immediately after flowering or autumn

Propagation: divide rhizomes keeping them near the surface

Species cultivated: many superb hybrids and garden varieties available (photograph)

Cultivation and uses: fragrant, dense growing, rhizomes help to exclude weeds. Lift and replant every third or fourth year, topdress with superphosphate of lime each spring, 25 to 55 g per sq m (1 to 2 oz per sq yd)

An iris rhizome

Red Hot Poker, Torch Lily
Kniphofia

Site: sunny

Soil: fertile, well drained in winter, but not liable to dry out when the flower spikes form

Height: 60 to 120 cm (2 to 4 ft)

Spread: depends on variety

Flowers: orange, yellow, cream, red

Flowering time: early summer to early autumn

Sowing time: spring

Planting time: spring

Propagation: sow seeds in a frame or greenhouse, transplant outdoors when large enough to handle; divide plants in spring

Species cultivated: many hybrids are available, some dwarf, some tall

Cultivation and uses: a useful plant in borders and island beds. Protect in severe winters by drawing leaves over the centre of the plant and tying them, and give a mulch of decayed manure or garden compost in spring. Leave undisturbed as long as possible

Blazing Star
Liatris

Site: sunny, open

Soil: light, fairly rich, not likely to dry out too much in summer

Height: up to 120 cm (4 ft)

Spread: up to 30 cm (1 ft)

Flowers: purple

Flowering time: summer

Planting time: spring; just cover roots with soil

Propagation: divide plants in spring; sow seed out of doors in early autumn or in cool greenhouse in spring

Species cultivated: *L. spicata alba*, white flowers, 60 cm (2 ft); *L. pycnostachya* 1.2 m (4 ft) purplish crimson flowers; *L. callilepsis*, reddish purple flowers in summer, 60 cm (2 ft) tall; 'Kobold' (photograph), is one of the most brilliant kinds, 60 cm (2 ft)

Cultivation and uses: good cut flowers; very beautiful border plants. Water freely in dry weather. Plants die back below ground level in winter

Giant Ragwort
Ligularia

Site: light shade or sun

Soil: moist, rich

Height: up to 2 m (6 ft)

Spread: 60 cm (2 ft)

Flowers: orange, yellow

Flowering time: early to late summer

Sowing time: spring, early summer

Planting time: spring or autumn

Propagation: divide plants in spring or autumn; sow seed outdoors and keep moist

Species cultivated: *L. dentata* (photograph), orange flowers in summer, 120 cm (4 ft); 'Gregynog Gold' large orange flowers in summer, 2 m (6 ft); *L. przewalskii*, yellow flowers in summer, 1.5 m (5 ft)

Uses: suitable for moist situations and planting beside pools; makes good ground cover

Lupin
Lupinus

Site: sunny, open

Soil: well drained, lime free, sandy

Height: up to 1.5 m (5 ft)

Spread: up to 60 cm (2 ft)

Flowers: white, cream, yellow, orange, pink, blue, violet, purple; scented

Flowering time: late spring to summer

Planting time: spring or autumn

Propagation: sow seeds outdoors in spring or as soon as ripe, transplant to flowering positions when large enough to handle; take cuttings of young growth in spring and root in sandy soil

Species cultivated: *L. polyphyllus* hybrids (photograph) up to 1.2 m (4 ft), flowers of various colours from late spring to early summer; the 'Russell Varieties' are the finest forms

Cultivation and uses: back of border planting, will produce self-sown seedlings if flowers are left. Not long lived, renew fairly frequently from seeds or cuttings

Campion
Lychnis

Site: sunny

Soil: light, fertile, well drained

Height: up to 90 cm (3 ft)

Spread: up to 45 cm (1½ ft)

Flowers: pink to crimson

Flowering time: summer

Sowing time: spring, early summer

Planting time: spring or autumn

Propagation: divide plants in spring; sow seeds in a sunny position outdoors, transplant in autumn to permanent position

Species cultivated: *L. coronaria* (photograph), 90 cm (3 ft); *L. coronaria alba*, white flowers; *L. chalcedonica*, Maltese cross, scarlet flowers borne in dense flat heads, late summer, 90 cm (3 ft) high; *L. flos-jovis*, bright pink flowers, 45 cm (1½ ft) tall

Cultivation and uses: can be grown on dry poor soil. Cut down flower stems in autumn unless self-sown seedlings are required; short lived; mulch every spring with compost or well-rotted manure

Loosestrife
Lysimachia

Site: sunny or shady

Soil: moist, ordinary

Height: up to 90 cm (3 ft)

Spread: up to 60 cm (2 ft)

Flowers: yellow, white

Flowering time: summer

Planting time: spring or autumn

Propagation: divide plants in spring or autumn; sow seeds outdoors in spring or early summer

Species cultivated: *L. clethroides*, white flowers, late summer, 90 cm (3 ft); *L. punctata* (photograph), yellow flowers, summer, 60 to 90 cm (2 to 3 ft); *L. nummularia* (creeping Jenny), trailing plant preferring damp places but will grow anywhere, yellow flowers, there is a golden-leaved form 'Aurea'

Cultivation and uses: easy to grow and may be invasive. Cut down flower stems in autumn

Purple Loosestrife
Lythrum

Site: sun or light shade

Soil: moist, ordinary

Height: up to 120 cm (4 ft)

Spread: up to 45 cm (1½ ft)

Flowers: magenta, pink

Flowering time: summer

Planting time: spring or autumn

Propagation: divide plants in spring or autumn

Species cultivated: *L. salicaria*, reddish-purple, 120 cm (4 ft), many hybrids are available; *L. virgatum*, pink, 90 cm (3 ft) and forms such as 'Rose Queen' and 'The Rocket'

Cultivation and uses: good for poolside planting. Cut back to ground level in autumn

Mallow
Malva

Site: sunny

Soil: reasonably drained, ordinary

Height: up to 120 cm (4 ft)

Spread: up to 60 cm (2 ft)

Flowers: shades of pink and white

Flowering time: summer to autumn

Planting time: spring or autumn

Propagation: divide plants in spring; take cuttings in spring or summer and root in a frame; sow seeds in spring in a frame or outdoors, transplant to flowering site in autumn

Species cultivated: *M. alcea* 'Fastigiata', (photograph) rose pink, 120 cm (4 ft); *M. moschata*, musk mallow, pink, 90 cm (3 ft) tall; the form *M. m. alba* has white flowers

Cultivation and uses: useful border flowers, do well and are longer lived on poor soils, long displays of flowers. Not usually very long lived; cut down stems in autumn

Himalayan Poppy
Meconopsis

Site: light shade, protected

Soil: light, rich and well drained but moist

Height: up to 1.5 m (5 ft)

Spread: up to 45 cm (1½ ft)

Flowers: blue, yellow, white, pink

Flowering time: summer

When to sow: late summer or early autumn, or as soon as ripe

Planting time: spring

Propagation: sow seeds in a greenhouse, transplant outside when small plants have formed

Species cultivated: *M. betonicifolia* (photograph) Himalayan poppy, to 120 cm (4 ft), blue flowers in early summer; *M. cambrica* (Welsh poppy), 30 cm (1 ft), yellow flowers in the summer, it likes a sunny position; *M. napaulensis* (satin poppy), 2 m (6 ft), blue, pink, purple or white flowers in the summer

Cultivation and uses: plants for the woodland garden; may need staking; water in summer if dry; cut down in autumn

Bergamot, Oswego Tea
Monarda

Site: sun or partial shade

Soil: moist

Height: up to 90 cm (3 ft)

Spread: up to 45 cm (1½ ft)

Flowers: pink, scarlet, mauve, white

Flowering time: summer

Sowing time: spring, early summer

Planting time: spring or autumn

Propagation: divide in spring or autumn; sow seeds in light soil in a partially shaded position outdoors, transplant in autumn

Species cultivated: *M. didyma*, to 90 cm (3 ft), scarlet, many garden varieties available such as 'Adam' rose red, 'Croftway Pink' pink, 'Croftway Scarlet' red

Cultivation and uses: aromatic leaves can be dried and used as a tea, sweetly scented flowers. Mulch with manure or compost each spring, cut down stems in autumn

Evening Primrose

Oenothera

Site: sunny

Soil: well drained, light, sandy

Height: up to 90 cm (3 ft)

Spread: up to 30 cm (1 ft)

Flowers: yellow, white

Flowering time: early summer to early autumn

Planting time: spring or autumn

Propagation: divide roots in spring; sow seeds outdoors in spring, transplant to flowering position in autumn

Species cultivated: *O. missouriensis*, 23 cm (9 in), yellow, sprawls well over the rock garden; *O. tetragona*, 45 cm (18 in), yellow, an upright plant for the border which has many good garden forms including 'Yellow River' and 'Fireworks'

Cultivation and uses: suitable for borders and informal gardens, the prostrate species make colourful ground cover. Cut back to ground level in autumn; may be short lived; lift and divide *tetragona* varieties every 3 years

Peony

Paeonia

Site: sun or light shade

Soil: fertile, well drained

Height: up to 90 cm (3 ft)

Spread: up to 90 cm (3 ft)

Flowers: yellow, white, red, maroon, pink, single or double

Flowering time: late spring to early summer

Planting time: autumn or spring

Propagation: divide roots in spring or autumn; sow seeds in a frame as soon as ripe or in spring

Species cultivated: *P. officinalis*, red, pink, or white, usually double flowers; *P. mlokosewitschii*, pale green leaves and single yellow flowers; *P. lactiflora*, white single flowers; many garden varieties are available in shades of pink, salmon and red

Cultivation and uses: for cutting, decorative foliage. Resent disturbance; mulch in spring with rotted manure or garden compost; water in dry weather

Poppy
Papaver

Site: sunny

Soil: deep, sandy, dryish

Height: up to 90 cm (3 ft)

Spread: up to 60 cm (2 ft)

Flowers: white, yellow, orange, pink, red or purple

Flowering time: late spring to early autumn

Planting time: spring or autumn

Propagation: divide plants in spring; take root cuttings and insert in frame or cool greenhouse in winter; sow seeds in a frame or sunny place outdoors in spring or early summer, transplant in autumn to permanent position

Species cultivated: *P. pilosum*, 90 cm (3 ft), scarlet and orange flowers, summer; *P. orientale*, 90 cm (3 ft); many hybrids (photograph) with orange, scarlet, pink, salmon, white, single or double flowers from late spring to early summer, 'Mrs Perry' salmon pink darker centre, 'Marcus Perry' orange red, 'King George' scarlet frilled

Cultivation and uses: seeds used in cooking; needs staking, dead head when flowering is over

Pennisetum
Pennisetum

Site: sunny and sheltered

Soil: well drained

Height: up to 1.5 m (5 ft)

Spread: up to 60 cm (2 ft)

Flowers: brown, green or purple spikes

Flowering time: midsummer to mid autumn

Sowing time: spring

Planting time: spring

Propagation: sow seeds in spring in 15 to 18°C (59 to 64°F); divide clumps in spring

Species cultivated: *P. setaceum* (fountain grass), 90 cm (3 ft), pale green spikes; *P. latifolium*, up to 1.5 m (5 ft), green spikes, needs protection in severe weather; *P. villosum* is best grown as an annual as it needs winter protection, it grows to 60 cm (2 ft) and has purple flower spikes

Cultivation and uses: these grasses can be dried and used in winter flower arrangements; distinctive border plants; they all require winter protection in cool climates as none is really hardy

Penstemon

Penstemon

Site: sunny

Soil: fertile and well drained

Height: up to 120 cm (4 ft)

Spread: up to 60 cm (2 ft)

Flowers: white, pink, violet, purple, scarlet, blue

Flowering time: late spring to early autumn

Planting time: spring

Propagation: sow seeds at 15 to 18°C (59 to 64°F) in spring, transplant outdoors in late spring or early summer; take cuttings late spring and insert in a frame; divide in spring

Species cultivated: *P. gloxinioides*, 60 cm (2 ft), many named varieties, usually grown as annuals as they are not always hardy enough to survive the winter in cool climates; *P. heterophyllus*, 23 cm (15 in), hardy, mauve or blue; *P. scouleri* (photograph), to 30 cm (12 in), rosy lilac

Cultivation and uses: bedding plants for the border and in the rock garden. Cut down stems in autumn; protect plants in winter with cloches or dry litter – this is unnecessary in frost-free climates

Phlox

Phlox

Site: sun or light shade

Soil: deep, fertile, not likely to dry out

Height: up to 120 cm (4 ft)

Spread: up to 90 cm (3 ft)

Flowers: white, mauve, pink, purple, red

Flowering time: early to late summer

Planting time: spring or autumn

Propagation: take root cuttings in winter and insert in a cool greenhouse or frame as a precaution against eelworm; divide plants in spring or autumn

Species cultivated: *P. maculata*, up to 90 cm (3 ft), white mauve, pink flowers; *P. paniculata*, up to 120 cm (4 ft), pink, red, lilac, purple or white flowers in summer, depending on variety (photograph)

Cultivation and uses: fragrant, cut flowers, some have variegated foliage, very good border plants. Cut down stems in autumn; lift, divide and replant in fresh soil every 2 to 3 years as plants are likely to become infected with eelworm – a soil-borne pest

Hart's-tongue Fern
Phyllitis

Site: shady

Soil: limy, humus rich

Height: up to 60 cm (2 ft)

Spread: up to 45 cm (18 in)

Planting time: spring

Propagation: sow spores on fine peat in well-drained pans and keep in cool greenhouse in spring or summer; divide plants in spring

Species cultivated: *P. scolopendrium*, up to 60 cm (2 ft); and variety 'Crispum' (photograph) with wavy edged fronds. 'Crispum' is sterile so increase by division or place the clean old frond bases in compost in pots covered with plastic until bulbils form. These will grow into plants and should be transplanted into pots after approximately one month. There are many other attractive varieties

Cultivation and uses: provides interesting greenery all the year; ideal for planting in old walls, between rocks and in shady borders. Water in dry weather

Chinese Lantern
Physalis

Site: sunny

Soil: well drained, rich

Height: up to 60 cm (2 ft)

Spread: up to 45 cm (18 in)

Flowers: insignificant, white, followed by inflated orange fruits which look like lanterns

Flowering time: summer

Planting time: spring

Propagation: divide plants in spring; sow seeds outdoors in spring or early summer, transplant in autumn to permanent position

Species cultivated: *P. alkekengi*, up to 30 cm (1 ft), *P. franchetii* (photograph), up to 60 cm (2 ft), with larger leaves and 'lanterns'

Cultivation and uses: dried lanterns used for winter flower arrangements. Lift, divide and replant in fresh soil every 3 years, can be invasive

Obedient Plant
Physostegia

Site: lightly shaded or sunny

Soil: fertile, not likely to dry out

Height: up to 90 cm (3 ft)

Spread: up to 60 cm (2 ft)

Flowers: white, also pink forms

Flowering time: summer to early autumn

Planting time: spring or autumn

Propagation: take cuttings in spring; divide plants in spring; take root cuttings in winter; sow seeds outdoors in spring

Species cultivated: *P. virginiana*, up to 120 cm (4 ft), pink flowers, not very effective. It has excellent varieties such as 'Alba' (photograph) to 90 cm (3 ft) and 'Vivid' rose pink flowers, to 60 cm (2 ft)

Cultivation and uses: handsome plant for borders and island beds. Mulch in spring, water well in dry weather; lift, divide and replant every 3 years

Cinquefoil
Potentilla

Site: sunny position

Soil: fertile, well drained

Height: up to 60 cm (2 ft)

Spread: up to 45 cm (18 in)

Flowers: white, cream, yellow, orange, pink, red

Flowering time: early summer to early autumn

Planting time: autumn

Propagation: sow seeds in a frame or outdoors in spring; divide plants – spring is best, or in autumn

Species cultivated: *P. nepalensis* hybrids up to 60 cm (2 ft), profuse flowering throughout summer, short lived, 'Miss Wilmott' (photograph), pink flowers, 'Roxana' orange red flowers; *P. atrosanguinea*, up to 60 cm (2 ft), is longer lived, crimson flowers throughout summer, has given rise to many hybrids with a range of flower colours, yellow, orange, pink, red, some two toned, some double

Cultivation and uses: suitable for hot dry borders; smaller kinds good in rock gardens. Cut back after flowering; mulch in spring; lift, divide and replant every 3 years

Lungwort

Pulmonaria

Site: partial or full shade

Soil: moist, fertile

Height: up to 45 cm (1½ ft)

Spread: up to 60 cm (2 ft)

Flowers: pink, blue, red, violet

Flowering time: spring, summer

Planting time: spring or autumn

Propagation: sow seeds in shady position outdoors in spring; divide in spring or autumn

Species cultivated: *P. angustifolia*, blue cowslip, pink flowers which turn blue, spring, up to 23 cm (9 in); *P. officinalis*, Jerusalem cowslip, lungwort, pink flowers becoming violet-blue, spring, up to 23 cm (9 in); *P. rubra*, brick red flowers in early spring, up to 23 cm (9 in); *P. saccharata* (photograph), Bethlehem sage, pink flowers turning to blue, spring, up to 30 cm (1 ft)

Cultivation and uses: good for ground cover as it provides decorative foliage and early flowers. Mulch in spring and water if the weather is dry. Lift and replant in fresh soil every 4 to 5 years

Pasque Flower

Pulsatilla

Site: sunny, open

Soil: well drained, fertile, good on chalk

Height: 30 cm (1 ft)

Spread: 30 cm (1 ft)

Flowers: white, pink, purple, yellow

Flowering time: spring

Planting time: spring

Propagation: sow seeds in a frame or greenhouse in spring, transplant to flowering position when very young; divide plants carefully in spring

Species cultivated: *P. vulgaris* (photograph), purple; it has a number of named varieties of other colours including 'Alba' white, 'Rubra' red and 'Mrs Van der Elst' pink; *P. alpina*, white flowers; *P. vernalis*, 15 cm (6 in), white flowers and its variety *sulphurea* with yellow flowers

Cultivation and uses: these dainty flowers with their feathery foliage can be used in the rock garden or scree bed. *P. a. sulphurea* should be grown in lime-free soil. Leave plants undisturbed once established

Rodgersia

Rodgersia

Site: sheltered and shady

Soil: moist, deep

Height: up to 1.5 m (5 ft)

Spread: up to 75 cm (2½ ft)

Flowers: cream or pink

Flowering time: summer

Planting time: spring, place the rhizomes 2.5 cm (1 in) below the surface

Propagation: divide the rhizomes (underground stems) in spring

Species cultivated: *R. aesculifolia*, to 120 cm (4 ft), pink flowers, bronze foliage; *R. podophylla*, to 90 cm (3 ft), cream flowers, bronze foliage; *R. tabularis*, to 90 cm (3 ft), cream flowers, bright green foliage

Cultivation and uses: grown for the sculptural foliage rather than the flowers, rodgersias grace any border or woodland garden; good poolside plants. Remove dead flowers; water in dry weather

Coneflower

Rudbeckia

Site: sunny, open

Soil: well drained but moist and fertile

Height: up to 2 m (6 ft)

Spread: up to 60 cm (2 ft)

Flowers: yellow, brown, orange

Flowering time: summer to early autumn

Planting time: spring or autumn

Propagation: sow seeds in a sunny place outdoors in spring or early summer (seedlings may be variable so division is better); divide clumps in autumn or in reasonable weather in winter

Species cultivated: *R. speciosa fulgida* (photograph) up to 60 cm (2 ft), yellow with a purple centre; *R. nitida*, up to 120 cm (4 ft), yellow with a green centre; a number of named varieties are available including Herbstonne, 2 m (6 ft)

Cultivation and uses: tall varieties useful for the backs of borders; all varieties make good cut flowers. Cut off dead flowers; cut stems down in autumn; lift, divide and replant every 3 years

Salvia
Salvia

Site: sunny

Soil: well drained, ordinary with added garden compost or rotted manure

Height: up to 120 cm (4 ft)

Spread: up to 60 cm (2 ft)

Flowers: white, purple, blue, red, yellow

Flowering time: summer to early autumn

Planting time: autumn or spring

Propagation: sow seeds outdoors in spring; divide roots in autumn or spring

Species cultivated: many good species and varieties, one of the best is *S.* × *superba*, up to 90 cm (3 ft), violet blue. This has a number of named varieties including 'East Friesland' (photograph)

Cultivation and uses: suitable for borders and island beds. Cut down stems to ground level in autumn; lift, divide and replant every 3 years

London Pride
Saxifraga

Site: sun or shade

Soil: moist, ordinary

Height: up to 45 cm ($1\frac{1}{2}$ ft)

Spread: up to 45 cm ($1\frac{1}{2}$ ft)

Flowers: white, cream, pink

Flowering time: early to midsummer

Planting time: spring

Propagation: divide clumps in spring; sow seeds in a greenhouse in spring; take cuttings of non-flowering parts in early summer

Species cultivated: *S. umbrosa* (photograph), up to 45 cm ($1\frac{1}{2}$ ft), pink flowers in summer; *S. u. primuloides*, a dwarf form up to 20 cm (8 in), deeper pink flowers; another form 'Variegata' has leaves marked with yellow

Cultivation and uses: smaller kinds for the rock garden; shiny, decorative rosettes of foliage make good ground or edging plants for the border. Easy to grow. Cut off dead flowers; divide when necessary

Scabious, Pincushion Flower
Scabiosa

Site: sunny, open

Soil: well drained, fertile, preferably with lime or chalk for *S. caucasica*

Height: up to 90 cm (3 ft)

Spread: up to 45 cm (1½ ft)

Flowers: blue, white, mauve, lilac

Flowering time: summer to early autumn

Planting time: spring

Propagation: divide clumps in spring; take 5-cm (2-in) long cuttings and insert in a peat/sand compost in spring

Species cultivated: *S. caucasica* (Caucasian scabious) (photograph), to 60 cm (2 ft), light blue; a number of named varieties are available including 'Clive Greaves' mauve, 'Miss Wilmott' white, and 'Lodden Anna' blue

Cultivation and uses: can be dried and used in flower arrangements; interesting border plant. Some staking may be necessary for the taller kinds; cut off dead flowers to encourage a second flowering; cut down to ground level in early winter; lift, divide and replant every 3 years

Stonecrop
Sedum

Site: sunny, rather dry

Soil: well drained, sandy

Height: up to 60 cm (2 ft)

Spread: up to 60 cm (2 ft)

Flowers: white, yellow, pink, red

Flowering time: summer to mid autumn

Planting time: autumn or spring

Propagation: sow seeds outdoors in spring; divide clumps in autumn or early spring; take cuttings in spring or summer and root in sandy soil

Species cultivated: *S. spectabile* (photograph), 45 cm (1½ ft), pink flowers in autumn, a number of named varieties are available; *S. maximum* 'Atropurpureum' up to 90 cm (3 ft), purple foliage and pink flowers; *S. spathulifolium*, 10 cm (4 in), a mat-forming species with yellow flowers; *S. acre*, 5 cm (2 in), mat forming with yellow flowers. A very handsome variety is 'Autumn Joy' to 60 cm (2 ft), pink flowers which turn to coppery red

Cultivation and uses: the low-growing species are suitable for the rock garden; foliage and flowers of all kinds are attractive; *S. spectabile* attracts butterflies. Prone to disease in wet soil; remove dead flower stems in spring

Sidalcea
Sidalcea

Site: sunny

Soil: well drained

Height: up to 120 cm (4 ft)

Spread: up to 60 cm (2 ft)

Flowers: pink, red

Flowering time: summer to early autumn

Planting time: spring or autumn

Propagation: sow seeds outdoors in spring or summer, but varieties will not come true from seed; divide in spring or autumn, replanting the outer parts of the clump

Species cultivated: many garden varieties of *S. malvaeflora* are available including 'Brilliant' (photograph) carmine, 'Oberon' pale pink, 'Rev. Page Roberts' shell pink, 'Rose Queen' rose, 'Loveliness' shell pink

Cultivation and uses: valuable plant for borders and island beds. May need protection during severe winters; lift, divide and replant every 3 years

Golden Rod
Solidago

Site: sun or light shade

Soil: ordinary, well drained

Height: up to 2.5 m (8 ft)

Spread: up to 60 cm (2 ft)

Flowers: yellow

Flowering time: summer to mid autumn

Planting time: spring or autumn

Propagation: varieties do not come true from seed so divide roots in spring or autumn

Species cultivated: very good array of garden hybrids which include 'Goldenmosa' to 90 cm (3 ft), 'Golden Thumb' to 30 cm (1 ft), 'Lemore' primrose flowers, to to 75 cm (2½ ft), 'Golden Wings' to 2 m (6 ft)

Cultivation and uses: good for providing height at the back of the border; can be used as cut flowers. Taller kinds need staking; cut down to ground level in late autumn; lift, divide and replant every 3 years

Lamb's Tongue, Lamb's Ear
Stachys

Site: sunny and sheltered

Soil: well drained, ordinary

Height: 45 cm (1½ ft)

Spread: 60 to 90 cm (2 to 3 ft)

Flowers: red, purple, pink

Flowering time: summer

Planting time: spring or autumn

Propagation: divide plants in spring or autumn

Species cultivated: *S. lanata*, to 45 cm (1½ ft), purplish red flowers, decorative woolly foliage; a number of named varieties are available including 'Silver Carpet' a non-flowering variety with silver foliage and 'Olympica' with magenta flowers and greyish-white foliage

Cultivation and uses: grown for its silvery, hairy foliage rather than for its flowers which should be removed to show the foliage at its best. Very good ground cover in the right conditions

Meadow Rue
Thalictrum

Site: sun or light shade

Soil: rich, well drained but slightly moist

Height: up to 2 m (6 ft)

Spread: up to 45 cm (1½ ft)

Flowers: mauve, purple, yellow, white

Flowering time: summer

Planting time: spring

Propagation: best increased by seeds sown in a frame or outdoors in spring; lift and divide carefully in spring

Species cultivated: *T. aquilegifolium*, 90 cm (3 ft), mauve flowers; *T. dipterocarpum* (photograph) 2 m (6 ft), rosy-mauve flowers with yellow anthers, its variety 'Album' has white flowers; *T. flavum*, 1.5 m (5 ft) yellow flowers, and variety 'Glaucum' with grey-green foliage; *T. rocquebrunianum*, 120 cm (4 ft), lavender-blue flowers

Cultivation and uses: grown for their elegant foliage as much as for their flowers. Taller varieties will need staking; cut down plants in autumn after flowering; topdress in spring with leafmould or garden compost; lift and divide only when essential – plants are better left undisturbed

Spiderwort

Tradescantia

Site: sun or light shade

Soil: well drained, ordinary

Height: 60 cm (2 ft)

Spread: 45 cm (1½ ft)

Flowers: white, blue, purple, pink; each lasts for one day only

Flowering time: summer to early autumn

Planting time: mid autumn or spring

Propagation: named varieties do not come true from seed so lift and divide clumps in spring or autumn

Species cultivated: *T. virginiana* has a number of named varieties which are most often cultivated including 'Caerulea' bright blue, 'Osprey' white with a blue eye, 'Rubra' dark pinkish red, 'Iris Prichard' pale violet

Cultivation and uses: good for town planting as it tolerates a polluted atmosphere. Cut down in autumn; lift, divide and replant every 3 or 4 years

Globe Flower

Trollius

Site: sun or light shade

Soil: deep, moist

Height: up to 90 cm (3 ft)

Spread: up to 45 cm (1½ ft)

Flowers: yellow, orange

Flowering time: mid spring to midsummer

Planting time: autumn or spring

Propagation: sow seeds outdoors in moist soil and a shady position in mid autumn or mid spring; divide plants in autumn or spring

Species cultivated: there are a number of named hybrids including 'Goldquelle' buttercup yellow, 'Earliest of All' lemon yellow, 'Orange Princess' orange yellow, 'Orange Globe' (photograph) orange yellow; *T. asiaticus* is orange and grows to 45 cm (1½ ft); *T. pumilus* has yellow flowers and grows to 30 cm (1 ft)

Cultivation and uses: can be planted at the margins of streams or ponds. Water well in dry weather; remove dead flowers to encourage a second crop; lift, divide and replant every 3 years

Mullein
Verbascum

Site: warm, sunny

Soil: well drained, deep and light

Height: up to 2 m (6 ft)

Spread: up to 60 cm (2 ft)

Flowers: white, cream, yellow, orange, pink, lilac, purple

Flowering time: early summer to mid autumn

Planting time: spring, autumn

Propagation: take root cuttings in spring and root in a greenhouse; increase the species by seeds sown in spring outdoors and transplanted to flowering positions in early autumn

Species cultivated: *V. phoeniceum*, purple mullein, 90 cm (3 ft), purple, violet, lilac, pink or white flowers, late spring to early autumn. Numerous garden varieties flowering from early to late summer: 'Pink Domino' 120 cm (4 ft), deep pink, 'Gainsborough' 120 cm (4 ft), yellow, grey foliage, 'Miss Wilmott' 2 m (6 ft), white. *V.* 'Golden Bush' 60 cm (2 ft), yellow, compact and bushy

Cultivation and uses: attractive border plants which are good for hot, dry places and poor soil. Stake if necessary; cut down in autumn after they have finished flowering

Speedwell
Veronica

Site: sunny or light shade

Soil: rich and well drained

Height: prostrate to 1.5 m (5 ft)

Spread: up to 60 cm (2 ft)

Flowers: blue, purple, pink, white

Flowering time: late spring to late summer

Planting time: spring or autumn

Propagation: divide in autumn or spring (the latter season is best); sow seeds in light soil outdoors in spring

Species cultivated: *V. teucrium*, 45 cm (1½ ft), blue, summer, and variety 'Royal Blue' (photograph), 60 cm (2 ft); *V. gentianoides*, 45 cm (1½ ft), light blue, spring and early summer; *V. longifolia*, 120 cm (4 ft), purple blue, all summer; *V. spicata*, 60 cm (2 ft), blue, summer, and hybrids 'Icicle' white, 'Minuet' pink, 'Sarabande' violet-blue

Cultivation and uses: taller kinds for the back of borders, smaller for the front or for rock gardens. Easily grown, cut down to ground level in late autumn; lift, divide and replant every 3 years

Pansy, Violet
Viola

Site: sun or partial shade

Soil: deep, rich

Height: up to 23 cm (9 in)

Spread: up to 30 cm (1 ft)

Flowers: maroon, purple, yellow, white, orange, blue, violet

Flowering time: late winter to mid autumn

Planting time: spring or autumn

Propagation: sow seeds outdoors in early summer and transplant to flowering positions in autumn (not all kinds come true from seed); divide plants in spring or autumn; take cuttings of non-flowering shoots in late summer and root in a shady frame

Species cultivated: good summer-flowering varieties include 'Avalanche' pure white, 'Arkwright Ruby' crimson, fragrant, 'Nora Leigh' (photograph) tufted flowers, Swiss Giants have masked flowers. Good winter-flowering varieties include 'Celestial Queen' light blue, 'Helios' yellow. *V. tricolor*, heartsease, 15 cm (6 in), dark blue to purple flowers from late spring to early autumn

Cultivation and uses: front of the border, cut flowers. Remove flowers as soon as they fade

Yucca
Yucca

Site: warm, sunny

Soil: sandy, light and well drained

Height: up to 2.5 m (8 ft)

Spread: up to 1.5 m (5 ft)

Flowers: white, cream

Flowering time: late summer to autumn

Planting time: spring or autumn

Propagation: take root cuttings in spring and insert in pots of sandy soil in 15 to 18°C (59 to 64°F); detach rooted suckers and offsets in spring

Species cultivated: *Y. filamentosa* (photograph), up to 1.5 m (5 ft), greyish-green foliage, creamy flowers in summer when plant is about 3 years old; *Y.f.* 'Variegata' has yellow stripes on the leaves but is less hardy; *Y. gloriosa*, up to 2.5 m (8 ft), creamy flowers in autumn produced when plants are about 5 years old, deep green rosette of leaves; *Y. recurvifolia*, up to 2.5 m (8 ft), creamy flowers in late summer and autumn but only carried on mature plants, has narrower leaves than *gloriosa*

Cultivation and uses: striking foliage, good as a specimen plant and in seaside gardens. Cut off dead flower spikes

Flowering Bulbs

The word 'bulb' is, of course, an omnibus term which in practice includes corms and tubers so far as the gardener is concerned. Between them such plants make an invaluable contribution to the garden, with some being ideal for naturalising in grass or woodland (things like the daffodils, crocuses, muscari and scillas) and others, like the garden tulips, being ideal for planting in beds. Many, too, can be grown in rock-garden settings – small tulips like the *Tulipa kaufmanniana* varieties, dwarf narcissi and irises, cyclamen and anemones like *Anemone blanda* and *A. apennina*. Then again there are those which need the protection of a warm, sunny wall bed to do well, *Sparaxis grandiflora* and *Tigridia pavonia*, for example; while others such as the brightly coloured tuberous begonias can only be grown outdoors, in the cooler climates, from late spring until the autumn, when the tubers must be brought indoors for storing overwinter.

With many gardens being on the small side these days it is not surprising that so much is made of growing bulbs in containers. So many of them, from daffodils and tulips to hyacinths and lilies, are excellent for this purpose. Naturally, you will suit the flower to the container but tubs give an enormous amount of scope for the bigger bulbs. It is amazing, too, what can be achieved with a few window boxes, whether in terms of daffodils, squills (scilla), glory of the snow (chionodoxa), tulips (the Early single and Early double kinds are especially good for this purpose), snowdrops (galanthus) or winter aconite (*Eranthis hyemalis*).

So much are dahlias considered as plants in their own right in gardening terms that it seems a little strange perhaps to include them in the community of bulbous plants – but there they belong with their tuberous roots. The dahlia is an indispensable plant whether one is thinking of the taller-growing decorative and cactus varieties or the low-growing bedding varieties. Not the least of the dahlia's merits is its excellence as a striking and long-lasting flower, and the more flowers which are cut the more the plants seem to produce.

Preparation for planting

Now for a few practical details. For some reason bulbs (and I'm again using the term in its broad sense) get less consideration with regard to soil conditions than most plants. It's a situation which should not be allowed to happen, for while it is perfectly true that the bulb is a storage organ containing its own supply of food, if it is going to continue to prosper it must have the wherewithal to build up reserves for the future. So, make sure that the soil is in good condition and well drained. The soil texture can be greatly improved by digging in peat or another form of organic matter and at the same time adding a dressing of bonemeal spread evenly on the surface at the rate of 110 g per sq m (4 oz per sq yd).

Planting

Always plant at the right time – autumn for the spring-flowering kinds, spring for the summer-flowering and those which are more tender – and at the right depth for the particular bulb (details of these are given in the individual plant notes), and with bulbs which are particularly susceptible to rotting, bed them on a lining of sharp sand. Lilies and gladioli are two which will do all the better for this attention.

When planting bulbs for naturalising, by far the best way to get a natural effect is to scatter handfuls around, planting them where they fall. Small quantities can, of course, be planted with a trowel but with larger numbers you really need a bulb-planting tool which will take out neatly a core of turf and soil to leave a planting hole. Place the bulb in position, replace the core of turf and soil and firm it in position with the foot. Again naturalised bulbs which have been in position for some time can be given a boost by dressing the ground in autumn with bonemeal at the rate of 110 g per sq m (4 oz per sq yd). A point to remember with all naturalised bulbs is that the grass around them should not be cut until the bulb foliage yellows and dies down.

In the case of bulbs grown in beds, it is again important that after they have flowered the foliage should be allowed to die back naturally. If the space is needed for other plants, or if the bulbs are likely to be damaged by frost, then they should be dug up carefully and planted side by side in a trench in another part of the garden until the leaves have died down. The bulbs can then be lifted, inspected for disease and the sound ones stored in trays in a frost-proof shed.

Bulbs in containers

When bulbs are grown in containers, the same need for good soil and good drainage applies. So, make sure first that the containers you intend to use have sufficient drainage holes in the base and that these are covered in turn with crocks (if you can still get hold of these now that plastic pots are so widely used) or small stones and then a layer of roughage such as fibrous pieces of peat. Then the soil can be added and I favour John Innes No. 1 potting compost for this purpose. Alternatively, use good garden soil mixed with peat and a dressing of bonemeal.

For house display it is usual to plant in bowls without drainage holes. With these it is better to use bulb fibre rather than ordinary composts. The fibre should be thoroughly moistened and the bulbs barely covered. Keep the bowls in a cool dark place for 8 to 10 weeks and then bring into a light room.

Increasing bulbs

Although most bulbs can be increased by seed, the seedlings take several years to flower and may often differ from the parent plants. It is better to use division of the bulb clusters as a method of increase – this varies with the type of 'bulb' as shown in the illustration opposite.

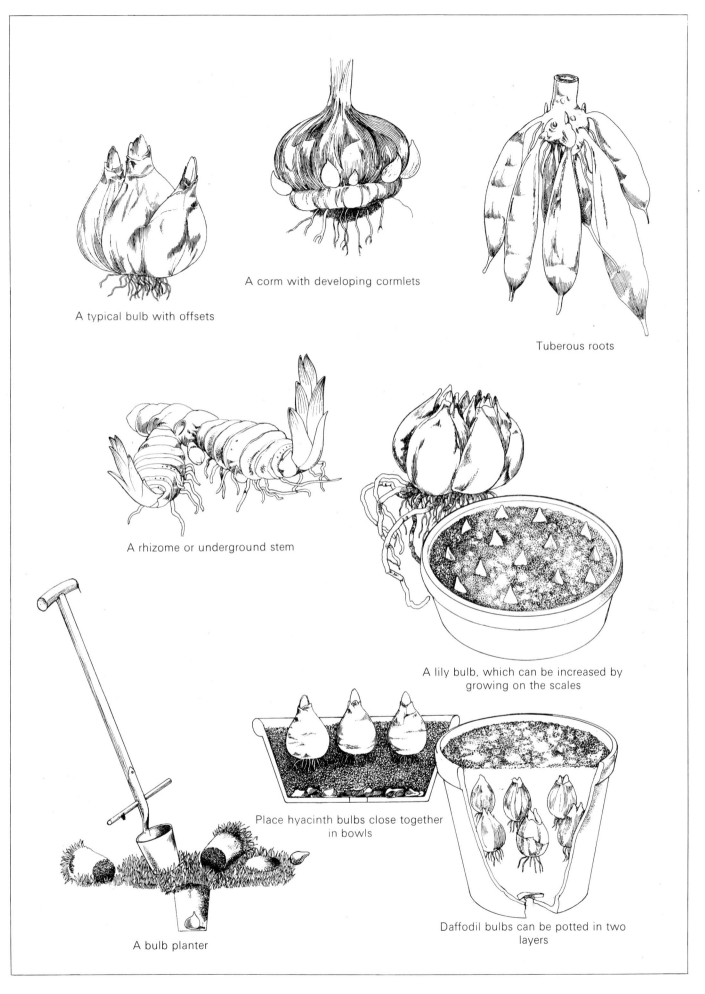

A typical bulb with offsets

A corm with developing cormlets

Tuberous roots

A rhizome or underground stem

A lily bulb, which can be increased by growing on the scales

A bulb planter

Place hyacinth bulbs close together in bowls

Daffodil bulbs can be potted in two layers

Allium

Allium

Site: sunny

Soil: well drained, ordinary

Height: 10 to 150 cm (4 in to 5 ft)

Type of plant: hardy bulb

Flowers: white, cream, pink, red, purple and violet blooms in sphere-like clusters

Flowering time: late spring to late summer

Planting time: mid to late autumn

Planting distance: 8 to 30 cm (3 to 12 in) depending on height of species; cover bulbs with twice their diameter of soil

Propagation: sow seeds in spring; lift clumps and replant the offsets

Species cultivated: many ornamental kinds available. *A. giganteum*, 120 cm (4 ft), is the one illustrated.

Cultivation and uses: water occasionally if very dry. Stake large flowers if necessary. Remove dead flowers but leave stems and leaves to die off naturally and then pull away. The leaves have the characteristic onion odour when bruised or crushed. They make striking border plants and the dried flower heads can be used for flower arranging

Windflower, Wood Anemone

Anemone

Site: sun or partial shade

Soil: well drained, preferably containing peat or leafmould

Height: 13 to 20 cm (5 to 8 in)

Type of plant: hardy tuberous-rooted perennial

Flowers: white, cream, purple, violet, pink, blue

Flowering time: late winter to spring

Planting time: autumn

Planting depth: 5 to 8 cm (2 to 3 in)

Propagation: sow seeds in spring outdoors or in pots of sandy soil; by natural increase of tubers

Species cultivated: *A. apennina*, blue, white or pink; *A. blanda* (photograph) blue, pink or white; *A. nemorosa*, white

Cultivation and uses: do not disturb; particularly effective if allowed to spread freely and naturalise. Picturesque under spring-flowering trees but flowers only open fully in the sun. Water when very dry. Allow flowers and leaves to die back naturally

Begonia

Begonia

Site: cool greenhouse or outdoors in a sheltered sunny or partially shady place. Will not survive frost

Soil: good, containing peat or leafmould

Height: 20 to 45 cm (8 to 18 in)

Type of plant: half-hardy tuberous-rooted perennial

Flowers: mostly double in white, cream, yellow, pink, orange, red

Flowering time: summer to autumn

Planting time: early spring

Planting distance: plant tubers hollow side up and an inch deep in boxes of moist peat in 15°C (59°F). Pot on when leaves start to grow. Plant outside when all risk of frost is past, spacing them 30 cm (12 in) apart

Propagation: take stem cuttings in spring and insert in propagator at 18°C (64°F)

Species cultivated: many good varieties of *B. × tuberhybrida* in a wide range of colours and forms (photograph)

Cultivation and uses: water well in summer but allow to dry off gradually in autumn. Wait until foliage turns yellow and then lift tubers, allow them to dry and store in a cool place. Feed pot-grown plants weekly in summer. Very good for bedding schemes in warmer areas or for use in window-boxes and containers

Quamash

Camassia

Site: sunny

Soil: moist

Height: 60 to 90 cm (2 to 3 ft)

Type of plant: hardy bulb

Flowers: white, blue, blue-violet

Flowering time: early summer

Planting time: autumn

Planting distance: 10 to 23 cm (4 to 9 in) apart and 10 cm (4 in) deep

Propagation: sow seeds in a sunny place outdoors or in pots in a temperature of 13°C (55°F); remove offsets from parent bulbs in autumn and replant

Species cultivated: *C. cusickii* (photograph), 90 cm (3 ft), light blue; *C. quamash*, 90 cm (3 ft), blue-violet to white

Cultivation and uses: topdress each year with leafmould, peat or garden compost. Water when the soil is dry. Leave plants undisturbed and lift and replant only when overcrowded. Unless the seeds are required, the dead flower heads can be removed. Plants grown from seed will take several years to flower

Canna

Canna

Site: sunny, in cooler climates the roots must be kept in a cool greenhouse over winter

Soil: rich, well manured or a ready mixed compost such as John Innes potting compost No. 2 or an equivalent soilless one

Height: 1 to 1.5 m (3 to 5 ft)

Type of plant: half-hardy, fleshy-rooted herbaceous perennial

Flowers: shades of orange, red, brown and crimson, sometimes attractively spotted

Flowering time: summer to early autumn

Planting time: winter or early spring with greenhouse protection in cool climates

Planting distance: pot up rhizomes in boxes and move to pots as the shoots grow. Plant outdoors 45 cm (18 in) apart once frost danger is past

Propagation: by division of the rhizomes; by seed soaked for 24 hours and sown in a temperature of 25°C (77°F) in late winter or spring

Species cultivated: there is a good range of garden varieties with either green (photograph) or purple foliage

Cultivation and uses: water well in dry weather and feed pot-grown plants with liquid fertiliser. Lift the roots in autumn once the foliage has been cut back by frost, clean them and store in boxes of barely damp soil until time for replanting. Spectacular summer bedding plant

Glory of the Snow

Chionodoxa

Site: sunny, good for rock gardens and window-boxes

Soil: well drained

Height: 15 cm (6 in)

Type of plant: hardy bulb

Flowers: white, pink or blue

Flowering time: spring

Planting time: autumn

Planting distance: 2.5 cm (1 in) apart, 8 cm (3 in) deep

Propagation: by seeds sown in light soil in summer; by offsets removed from parent bulbs

Species cultivated: *C. luciliae*, blue and white; *C. sardensis* (photograph), deep blue

Cultivation and uses: lift and replant every 3 years or so. They make attractive subjects for pot culture; plant 10 bulbs in a 13-cm (5-in) pot, cover and keep outdoors until well rooted and then bring indoors

Meadow Saffron
Colchicum

Site: sun or light shade

Soil: well drained, light with added peat

Height: 10 to 30 cm (4 to 12 in)

Type of plant: hardy bulb

Flowers: white, pink, purple

Flowering time: early to late autumn

Planting time: late summer

Planting distance: 8 cm (3 in) apart and 8 cm (3 in) deep

Propagation: sow seeds in sandy soil in summer outdoors or under glass. Also by division of the clumps at planting time

Species cultivated: *C. speciosum* and its varieties (photograph) pink, white, purple, 23 to 30 cm (9 to 12 in); *C. autumnale* and its varieties are smaller – 13 cm (5 in) or so. There are also double-flowered kinds

Cultivation and uses: the leaves die back in early summer before the flowers appear and do not reappear until the spring. There is no need to lift and replant. Can be naturalised in grass and are also good for rock gardens

Lily of the Valley
Convallaria

Site: cool, shady

Soil: moist, with added peat or leafmould

Height: 15 to 20 cm (6 to 8 in)

Type of plant: hardy, fleshy-rooted herbaceous perennial

Flowers: white or pink, fragrant

Flowering time: spring

Planting time: autumn

Planting distance: 5 to 8 cm (2 or 3 in) apart with the points of the crowns just below the surface

Propagation: sow seeds outdoors in spring; divide the roots in autumn or spring

Species cultivated: *C. majalis* white and *C. m. rosea* pink

Cultivation and uses: topdress with decayed manure or garden compost in late winter but do not disturb the roots. Roots can be forced by planting the crowns in shallow boxes, covering with peat and an inverted box until the flowers appear and then keeping in a warm light place. Makes good ground cover

Montbretia
Crocosmia

Site: sun or light shade, preferably near a wall

Soil: ordinary or sandy, good drainage

Height: 60 to 90 cm (2 to 3 ft)

Type of plant: hardy corm

Flowers: arching sprays of orange-red

Flowering time: late summer to early autumn

Planting time: spring

Planting distance: 15 cm (6 in) apart, 8 to 10 cm (3 to 4 in) deep

Propagation: by offsets removed from around the old corms

Species cultivated: many varieties of *C. crocosmiiflora* (photograph)

Cultivation and uses: in very frosty areas, lift the corms in late autumn and store them in a frost-proof shed. Otherwise leave in the ground but protect with bracken or straw in cold weather. Cut the old foliage back to ground level in spring. Lift and divide clumps every few years after flowering or in spring. Good border plant

Crocus
Crocus

Site: sunny, or light shade

Soil: well drained but rich

Height: 10 to 20 cm (4 to 8 in)

Type of plant: hardy corm

Flowers: white to yellow, blue, purple; some kinds attractively marked with stripes

Flowering time: autumn, late winter to spring

Planting time: spring-flowering kinds in autumn; autumn-flowering kinds in late summer

Planting distance: 8 cm (3 in) apart, 8 cm (3 in) deep

Propagation: by division of the corms in late summer

Species cultivated: many species and garden varieties available. The illustration is of the variety Pickwick

Cultivation and uses: leave undisturbed for 5 years or so and then lift and divide if necessary. Do not remove foliage until it turns yellow. For growing in pots, plant up in autumn 10 corms in a 15-cm (6-in) pot. Keep covered and cool until the shoots appear and then bring indoors. Small bulbs ideal as edgings to borders and in rock gardens

Cyclamen

Cyclamen

Site: shady, sheltered

Soil: peaty

Height: 10 to 15 cm (4 to 6 in)

Type of plant: hardy and half-hardy tuberous-rooted perennials

Flowers: pink to crimson and white

Flowering time: late winter, spring, summer, autumn

Planting time: early autumn

Planting distance: 5 to 8 cm (2 to 3 in) apart, 4 cm (1½ in) deep

Propagation: by seeds sown in pots in autumn and kept in a frame, transplant in spring

Species cultivated: *C. coum*, 10 cm (4 in), pink or white flowers in late winter and early spring; *C. neapolitanum*, 15 cm (6 in), red or white flowers in summer or autumn; *C. europaeum*, 15 cm (6 in), deep pink flowers in summer and early autumn; *C. repandum*, 10 cm (4 in) crimson flowers in spring. Some kinds have handsome marbled foliage

Cultivation and uses: topdress with decayed manure or compost after the leaves die down but do not cover the tubers. Water if very dry. Make pretty ground cover in thin woodland

Dahlia

Dahlia

Site: sunny, open

Soil: ordinary but with added manure or compost

Height: 25 cm to 2.5 m (10 in to 8 ft)

Type of plant: half-hardy tuberous-rooted perennial

Flowers: all shades of yellow, orange, red, pink, purple, mauve plus white

Flowering time: late summer to autumn

Sowing time: late winter in a heated greenhouse, mid spring in a frame, outdoors in late spring

Planting time: late spring after danger of frost is past

Planting distance: 45 to 90 cm (1½ to 3 ft) depending on height of variety, 8 cm (3 in) deep

Propagation: bedding kinds by seed; others by division of tubers or by cuttings from tubers potted up in late winter and brought on in a temperature of 15°C (59°F)

Species cultivated: there are numerous varieties in a great range of colour and flower forms

Cultivation and uses: water well when dry. Feed when flower buds appear. Support larger kinds with stout stakes. Remove dead flowers. Once foliage has been blackened by frost, cut it back, dig up the tubers and store them in a frost-free shed. In frost-free climates the tubers may be left in the ground in winter. Good border plants

Winter Aconite

Eranthis

Site: sunny or lightly shaded borders

Soil: ordinary

Height: 5 to 10 cm (2 to 4 in)

Type of plant: hardy tuberous-rooted perennial

Flowers: single, yellow with a ruff of green bracts

Flowering time: late winter to early spring

Planting time: autumn

Planting distance: 5 cm (2 in) apart and 5 cm (2 in) deep

Propagation: by division of tubers in autumn

Species cultivated: most usually grown is E. *hyemalis* (photograph), 8 to 10 cm (3 to 4 in), E. × *tubergenii*, 10 cm (4 in) is a more robust hybrid

Cultivation and uses: leave tubers undisturbed in the ground as long as possible. Water in spring if very dry. Makes attractive ground cover beneath deciduous trees and shrubs

Dog's-tooth Violet, Trout Lily

Erythronium

Site: semi-shade, rock gardens or borders

Soil: moist, containing peat or leafmould

Height: 15 to 45 cm (6 to 18 in)

Type of plant: hardy bulb

Flowers: white, cream, pink, mauve, purple or yellow

Flowering time: spring

Planting time: late summer to autumn

Planting distance: 10 to 15 cm (4 to 6 in) apart, 8 cm (3 in) deep

Propagation: remove offsets from bulbs and replant; sow seeds in summer and keep shaded and moist

Species cultivated: E. *dens-canis*, 15 to 23 cm (6 to 9 in), white, purple or pink; E. *revolutum*, 20 to 30 cm (8 to 12 in), rose-pink or white, mottled leaves; E. *tuolumnense*, 23 to 30 cm (9 to 12 in), golden yellow

Cultivation and uses: topdress after flowering with peat, leafmould or decayed manure. Leave bulbs undisturbed as long as possible. Water if very dry. Will grow under shrubs provided the soil does not dry out

Crown Imperial

Fritillaria imperialis

Site: sun or semi-shade

Soil: heavy, fairly rich

Height: 60 to 90 cm (2 to 3 ft)

Type of plant: hardy bulb

Flowers: striking heads of orange-red or yellow bell-shaped flowers

Flowering time: mid spring

Planting time: early to mid autumn

Planting distance: 30 cm (12 in) apart, 15 cm (6 in) deep

Propagation: remove offsets at planting time; sow seeds in early autumn in pots and overwinter in a cool, frost-free place

Species cultivated: there are a number of good varieties such as 'Aurora' deep red-orange, 'Lutea' (photograph), deep yellow, 'Rubra' orange

Cultivation and uses: do not transplant more frequently than every 4 years. Avoid cultivating around bulbs. Topdress annually with decayed manure or peat. The bulb is better if planted on its side to prevent water settling in the hollow top and rotting it. Striking border plants

Snake's-head Fritillary

Fritillaria meleagris

Site: semi-shade, will naturalise in short turf

Soil: moist, well drained

Height: 30 to 45 cm (12 to 18 in)

Type of plant: hardy bulb

Flowers: chequered bells in various shades of purple, also white

Flowering time: spring

Planting time: early autumn

Planting distance: 10 to 15 cm (4 to 6 in) apart, 10 cm (4 in) deep

Propagation: take off offsets at planting time; sow seeds in early autumn in pots and overwinter in a cool, frost-free place

Species cultivated: good forms of *F. meleagris* (photograph) include 'Aphrodite' white, 'Charon' dark purple, 'Saturnus' reddish purple

Cultivation and uses: do not transplant more often than once every 4 years. Plant the bulbs on their sides. If naturalised, the grass should not be mown before the foliage dies back

Snowdrop
Galanthus

Site: sun or semi-shade

Soil: good, moist

Height: 15 to 30 cm (6 to 12 in)

Type of plant: hardy bulb

Flowers: white bells with green markings

Flowering time: late winter to early spring

Planting time: autumn

Planting distance: 5 cm (2 in) apart and 2.5 cm (1 in) deep

Propagation: lift and divide clumps immediately after flowering. Sow seeds as soon as ripe in pots and keep cool and shaded

Species cultivated: *G. nivalis*, common snowdrop, (photograph) and its garden forms. *G. byzantinus* and *G. plicatus* are taller than *nivalis*; *G. ikariae* is slightly later flowering

Cultivation and uses: snowdrops planted as dry bulbs may take a year or so to establish themselves. When dividing clumps, do not let the bulbs dry out. Use in rock gardens or as an edging to a border

Gladiolus
Gladiolus

Site: sunny

Soil: rich, well manured and well drained

Height: 30 cm to 1.5 m (1 to 5 ft)

Type of plant: half-hardy corm

Flowers: pink, yellow, orange, red, purple, violet, and white

Flowering time: early summer to early autumn

Sowing time: spring

Planting time: early spring, by planting in succession the flowering period is prolonged. In frost-free climates, the corms are best planted in late autumn and winter

Planting distance: 15 to 20 cm (6 to 8 in) apart, 10 cm (4 in) deep

Propagation: by seeds sown in 15°C (59°F); by cormels pulled away from the base of the corms and planted in spring

Species cultivated: many varieties falling into groups divided up according to flower types, e.g. large flowered, miniatures, primulinus (hooded flowers) and butterfly

Cultivation and uses: add fertiliser at planting time; must not dry out in summer. Stake the hybrid kinds. Lift plants six weeks or so after the flowers fade, cut off top growth to within an inch of the corms and store these in an airy frost-proof place. Decorative border plants

Hyacinth

Hyacinthus

Site: sun or semi-shade, borders, window-boxes

Soil: well drained, rich

Height: 20 to 30 cm (8 to 12 in)

Type of plant: hardy bulb

Flowers: red, pink, blue, yellow and white, scented, bell shaped

Flowering time: spring, winter if forced

Planting time: autumn

Planting distance: 20 cm (8 in) apart and 8 to 10 cm (3 to 4 in) deep outdoors; 2.5 cm (1 in) apart and to half their depth in bowls or pots for indoor use

Propagation: sow seeds outdoors in autumn; remove offsets and plant in autumn

Species cultivated: many good varieties derived from *H. orientalis* including Delft Blue, Jan Bos, red, Pink Pearl, L'Innocence, white, City of Haarlem, yellow

Cultivation and uses: feed with bonemeal after planting. Protect with a covering of peat. Lift and dry bulbs after flowering – store in a cool place until planting time. Specially treated bulbs are available for forcing indoors. Keep pot-grown bulbs in a cool dark place until the flower spikes are visible and then bring indoors

Ipheion, Brodiaea

Ipheion

Site: warm, sunny, sheltered – good for rock gardens. Killed by heavy frosts

Soil: ordinary, well drained

Height: 15 to 20 cm (6 to 8 in)

Type of plant: fairly hardy bulb

Flowers: white, blue or lilac, star shaped

Flowering time: spring

Planting time: autumn

Planting distance: 8 cm (3 in) apart, 5 cm (2 in) deep

Propagation: lift when leaves die back, remove offsets and replant immediately

Species cultivated: *I. uniflorum* (photograph), white or lilac and the variety 'Coeruleum' light blue

Cultivation and uses: lift, divide and replant every 3 years or so. Good cut flowers

Iris, Spanish, Dutch, English
Iris

Site: sunny

Soil: ordinary, well drained with some lime

Height: 45 to 60 cm (1½ to 2 ft)

Type of plant: hardy bulb

Flowers: white, blue and mauve, yellow

Flowering time: late spring, early summer

Planting time: mid to late autumn

Planting distance: 15 cm (6 in) apart, 8 cm (3 in) deep

Propagation: sow seeds in pots in late summer or spring; remove offsets from the parent bulb

Species cultivated: there is a range of varieties of each of these groups. The Dutch iris (photograph) flower first, followed by the Spanish and then the English

Cultivation and uses: add bonemeal to soil before planting. Lift the Spanish and English irises every third year and replant. Cut off dead flowers but leave the foliage to die back before removing. These iris can also be forced into flower in pots or boxes in a greenhouse. Pot in autumn and water freely once growth appears. Dry off when the leaves wither. Good cut flowers

Snowflake
Leucojum

Site: sunny or semi-shady

Soil: fertile, moist for *L. aestivum* and *vernum*; well drained for *L. autumnale, roseum*

Height: 15 to 45 cm (6 to 18 in)

Type of plant: hardy bulb

Flowers: white or pink, similar to snowdrops

Flowering time: *L. vernum* in early spring, *aestivum* in late spring; *autumnale* and *roseum* in autumn

Planting time: late summer for *autumnale, roseum*; early autumn for *aestivum, vernum*

Planting distance: 10 cm (4 in) apart and 8 cm (3 in) deep

Propagation: remove offsets and replant in autumn; sow seeds in pots in spring

Species cultivated: summer snowflake, *L. aestivum* (photograph), white and green, 45 cm (18 in); *L. autumnale*, white and pink, 15 to 20 cm (6 to 8 in); *L. roseum*, pink, 10 cm (4 in); *L. vernum*, spring snowflake, white and green, 30 cm (12 in)

Cultivation and uses: leave undisturbed, lift and replant only very occasionally. Bulbs may not flower in the first year after planting. Plant in rock gardens or woodlands or naturalise in grass

Lily

Lilium

Site: dappled sunlight, shade for roots; half-hardy species in a cool greenhouse in cool climates

Soil: deep, containing peat or leafmould, well drained in winter

Height: 60 cm to 2.25 m (2 to 7 ft)

Type of plant: hardy and half-hardy bulbs

Flowers: yellow, orange, pink to crimson, white

Flowering time: mid spring to early autumn

Sowing time: spring

Planting time: autumn, as soon as bulbs are obtained

Planting distance: 15 to 25 cm (6 to 10 in) apart and 10 to 20 cm (4 to 8 in) deep

Propagation: divide bulb clusters at planting time; some species by seed, some by detaching bulb scales and potting these up

Species cultivated: many species and varieties, look for *L. regale*, white, one of the easiest; *L. tigrinum*, tiger lily, orange; *L. henryi*, orange; *L. auratum*, white spotted with yellow; *L. speciosum* (photograph) pinkish-white, spotted

Cultivation and uses: do not damage basal roots when planting. Mulch with peat or leafmould. Water in dry weather. Do not remove flower stems until the leaves turn yellow.

Grape Hyacinth

Muscari

Site: sunny

Soil: ordinary, well drained

Height: 15 to 45 cm (6 to 18 in)

Type of plant: hardy bulb

Flowers: blue, violet, also white

Flowering time: spring

Planting time: autumn

Planting distance: 10 cm (4 in) apart and 8 cm (3 in) deep

Propagation: sow seeds in a frame or outdoors in summer or spring; remove offsets or divide bulb clusters in late summer or autumn

Species cultivated: *M. armeniacum* (photograph) and several varieties mostly 20 cm (8 in); *M. botryoides album*, white, 15 cm (6 in); *M. tubergenianum*, dark and light blue, 20 cm (8 in)

Cultivation and uses: remove dead flowers unless required for seed, allow foliage to die back naturally. Lift and divide when overcrowded. Useful for rock gardens, or naturalising in grass

Daffodil
Narcissus

Site: sunny or slightly shaded

Soil: best in rich moist soils but very tolerant

Height: 8 to 60 cm (3 in to 2 ft)

Type of plant: hardy bulb

Flowers: white, cream, pink, yellow or orange, with many colour combinations

Flowering time: spring

Planting time: late summer or early autumn

Planting distance: 10 to 20 cm (4 to 8 in) apart and 10 to 15 cm (4 to 6 in) deep for larger kinds, 5 to 8 cm (2 to 3 in) deep and apart for small species

Propagation: remove offsets from parent bulbs and replant in late summer; sow seeds in sandy soil as soon as ripe

Species cultivated: daffodils are divided into groups according to flower type. In some the trumpet or cup is greatly reduced in size to form a small frill in the centre of the flower

Cultivation and uses: dust soil with bonemeal before planting. Cut off dead flowers but allow foliage to die back before removing. If naturalised, grass must not be cut until the leaves have turned yellow. Lift and replant only when flower quality deteriorates. Useful for growing in pots; the smaller species are best in rock gardens

Star of Bethlehem
Ornithogalum

Site: sunny, warm, sheltered

Soil: sandy, well drained

Height: up to 45 cm (1½ ft)

Type of plant: hardy and slightly tender bulbs

Flowers: silver-grey, white, yellow

Flowering time: late spring to summer

Planting time: hardy varieties from early to late autumn, tender kinds in mid spring

Planting distance: 15 cm (6 in) apart and 8 to 10 cm (3 to 4 in) deep

Propagation: remove offsets from old bulbs and replant

Species cultivated: *O. umbellatum*, Star of Bethlehem, white, 25 to 30 cm (10 to 12 in); *O. nutans*, silver-grey, 15 to 23 cm (6 to 8 in); *O. thyrsoides*, Chincherinchee, white, 38 cm (15 in) slightly tender

Cultivation and uses: topdress in spring with peat or leafmould. In cool climates lift the tender kinds in autumn and store dry in a frost-proof place until spring, or grow in pots in the conservatory throughout the year. Divide hardy kinds only when overcrowded

Striped Squill

Puschkinia

Site: sunny, partial shade

Soil: light, well drained

Type of plant: hardy bulb

Height: 10 to 20 cm (4 to 8 in)

Flowers: white or pale blue striped with blue

Flowering time: spring

Planting time: autumn

Planting distance: 5 to 8 cm (2 to 3 in) apart, 5 cm (2 in) deep

Propagation: sow seeds as soon as ripe in sandy soil in a cool greenhouse; remove offsets from old bulbs and replant in autumn

Species cultivated: *P. scilloides* (photograph) pale blue, and its varieties 'Compacta' and 'Alba' (white)

Cultivation and uses: lift, divide and replant when overcrowded. Allow foliage to die back naturally, remove flowers when faded if seed is not required. Grow in the rock garden or in pots in a cool greenhouse

Ranunculus

Ranunculus

Site: sunny, sheltered

Soil: light, moist, well drained

Height: 15 to 30 cm (6 to 12 in)

Type of plant: hardy tuberous-rooted perennial

Flowers: double or semi-double in white, cream and shades of orange, yellow, pink, crimson and purple

Flowering time: late spring to early summer

Planting time: late winter or early spring, also in autumn in frost-free places

Planting distance: 8 to 15 cm (3 to 6 in) apart, 5 cm (2 in) deep

Propagation: sow seeds in autumn in pots; divide the clusters of tubers

Species cultivated: garden varieties derived from *R. asiaticus* (photograph)

Cultivation and uses: plant the tubers with the claws downwards. Water well in dry weather; feed with liquid fertiliser in late spring and summer. In all but frost-free climates lift the tubers when the leaves turn yellow, dry them in the sun and store in a cool frost-free place until planting time. Good border plants

Squill

Scilla

Site: sunny, rock gardens or borders

Soil: sandy, deep

Height: 15 to 30 cm (6 to 12 in)

Type of plant: hardy bulb

Flowers: blue and lilac, also white and pink

Flowering time: late winter to early summer

Planting time: autumn

Planting distance: 10 cm (4 in) apart and 5 to 10 cm (2 to 4 in) deep

Propagation: sow seeds in sandy soil in summer or spring; remove offsets from old bulbs in autumn

Species cultivated: *S. biflora*, 15 cm (6 in), blue, early spring, also white and pink forms; *S. peruviana*, 15 to 30 cm (6 to 12 in), lilac, late spring to early summer; *S. sibirica* (photograph), 8 to 15 cm (3 to 6 in), blue, early spring

Cultivation and uses: lift, divide and replant when overcrowded. *S. peruviana* is slightly tender and good for growing in containers

Harlequin Flower

Sparaxis

Site: sunny, sheltered border or in pots in a frost-proof greenhouse

Soil: light, fertile, sandy

Height: 30 to 45 cm (12 to 18 in)

Type of plant: slightly tender corm

Flowers: carried several to a stem, orange, yellow, red, pink or purple (several colours to each flower)

Flowering time: spring

Planting time: autumn

Planting distance: 15 cm (6 in) apart and 5 cm (2 in) deep

Propagation: sow seeds in 15 to 18°C (59 to 64°F) in spring; divide the corm clusters in autumn

Species cultivated: *S. tricolor* and its varieties (photograph) are the kinds mostly grown

Cultivation and uses: in cool climates, cover the bulbs with straw in winter to give frost protection; or, lift when the leaves die, dry off and store in a frost-free place until planting time. When grown in pots, plant up in late summer or early autumn. Water sparingly and then more freely when the leaves show. Dry off after flowering

Tiger Flower
Tigridia

Site: warm, sunny, sheltered, or in pots in a cool greenhouse

Soil: fertile, draining well in winter but moist in summer

Height: 45 to 60 cm (18 to 24 in)

Type of plant: slightly tender bulb

Flowers: white, scarlet, purple, yellow, some blotched with another colour. Each bloom lasts for one day but they are produced in succession

Flowering time: midsummer to early autumn

Planting time: spring

Planting distance: 10 cm (4 in) apart and 8 to 10 cm (3 to 4 in) deep

Propagation: sow seeds in spring in 15 to 18°C (59 to 64°F); remove offsets and replant in spring

Species cultivated: *T. pavonia* (photograph), yellow and purple and its varieties such as 'Alba' white with red spots, 'Liliacea' reddish-purple with white markings, 'Lutea' yellow

Cultivation and uses: water freely if dry in summer. In winter in cool climates cover with straw or cloches or lift and store in a frost-proof shed until spring. For growing in pots, plant up in spring, water sparingly at first then moderately. Feed occasionally. Stop watering gradually when flowering is finished and store during winter

Tulip
Tulipa

Site: open, sunny or partial shade

Soil: light, fertile with added manure or garden compost

Height: 10 to 75 cm (4 to 30 in)

Spread: 15 to 20 cm (6 to 8 in)

Flowers: shades of pink, red, yellow, orange, purple, violet and white; some mottled or streaked

Flowering time: late winter to late spring

Planting time: autumn

Planting distance: 15 to 20 cm (6 to 8 in) apart and 10 cm (4 in) deep

Propagation: sow seeds in a frame in sandy soil in spring; remove offsets from parent bulb when foliage has died down

Species cultivated: there are a large number of species, also many garden varieties divided in groups such as Early single, Early double, Parrot, Rembrandt, Lily-flowered, Mendel, Triumph and Darwin

Cultivation and uses: mulch with compost or decayed manure. When foliage dies, either lift bulbs and store in the cool and dry until replanting or leave them in the ground and lift and divide once every 3 years or so. Bulbs may also be grown in pots for flowering indoors

Flowers from Seed

If you think that growing plants from seed is the most satisfying aspect of gardening then you could be right. It involves skill, even with the easiest subjects, and there are few greater thrills than to see seedlings one has nursed develop into strong, healthy, mature plants.

So, grouped together in this chapter you will find a selection of decorative flowering plants which will bring much pleasure and joy, mostly hardy or half-hardy annuals (or plants grown as such) with some biennials and perennials of real value. (See p. 7 for an explanation of these terms.)

But first the annuals, which have so many advantages as garden flowers. For a start they grow well on poorer soils, tending to make too much leafy growth at the expense of flowering if they are given a very rich growing medium. Ideal conditions are a light, well-drained soil and plenty of sunshine. Then there is the great advantage that you can make a real splash of colour for a relatively small outlay, and you can ring the changes if you want each year by experimenting with different colour schemes and varying the plants used. Mind you, if the soil is very poor then I would advise giving the ground a light dressing of bonemeal a few weeks before the seed is sown. This will be taken up slowly by the plants throughout the growing season.

What is of overriding importance is to work the soil down to a good tilth before sowing in the open ground. That, of course, is for the sowing of hardy annuals, which are sown in spring (between early and late spring depending on where you live and how cold it is), or, in some cases in late summer. Very hardy types can be sown at that later time to provide plants which will flower in late spring and early summer the following year.

Sowing

What is most necessary is to sow *thinly* for to do otherwise means that the seedlings suffer intense competition and, apart from this, it is very wasteful. However, to sow thinly is often easier said than done. Again, I prefer to sow in prepared seed drills (the depth depends on the seed being sown) rather than scattering the seeds over the soil as it makes thinning and weeding much easier. A useful tip when handling and sowing very fine seeds is to mix them with a small amount of sharp sand and then sprinkle the mixture finely along the drills.

Fill in the drills by raking over them lightly, the most shallowly-sown seeds will then have just the thinnest of soil coverings while others may be covered by 3.5 to 5 cm (1½ to 2 in) of soil. Make the first thinning of the seedlings which result as soon as they can be handled, and the final thinning several weeks later.

Now to turn to half-hardy annuals, which include lovely things like the petunias, antirrhinums, nemesias and lobelias, as well as the African and French marigolds.

None of these can be planted out until all danger of frost has passed. Seeds can be sown from late winter onwards in boxes or pots in a heated greenhouse (see pp. 8–9) the timing depending on the amount of heat you can provide. What you must be able to do is to provide a daytime temperature of about 13°C (55°F) and sowing can be left until as late as mid-spring if necessary. In addition, some half-hardy annuals can be sown in the open ground in late spring but they will, of course, be much later in flowering.

I like to get seeds of *Begonia semperflorens*, petunias, nicotianas, salvias, lobelias, antirrhinums and verbenas sown in the greenhouse by late winter and African and French marigolds, nemesias, cosmeas, asters and stocks in early spring.

The young plants so raised must be 'hardened off' for planting out in the garden after the last frosts. 'Hardening off' means that the young plants are placed in a frame and given increasing amounts of ventilation over a period of a couple of weeks. For the last few days all protection is removed unless there is a danger of frost. This accustoms the plants to the cooler weather out of doors.

Biennials and perennials are sown in a prepared seed bed in late spring or early summer with the resulting seedlings being transplanted to a nursery bed in midsummer and to their permanent quarters in the autumn or the following spring.

Planting

When planting either your own home-raised annuals or those bought in from a nursery, use a trowel and try to keep as much soil as possible round the roots. The tips of the plants should be removed to encourage the growth of side shoots which will result in bushier better looking plants.

Flowers grown from seed can be invaluable for container display and for this I like to choose plants such as the very colourful nasturtiums, petunias and calendulas (marigolds). For the owner of the small garden this can be a way to make a wonderful splash of colour in a small area, with the container-grown plants supplementing those in beds and clothing walls.

Aftercare

Water all plants freely in dry weather, paying especial attention to those grown in containers, and remove all weeds regularly by hoeing or handweeding.

Unless the seed is required, take off the faded flowers before the seed has a chance to form as this will encourage the plants to continue growing and flowering. Some annuals renew themselves from self-sown seed; a fact which may be useful or may be a nuisance according to circumstances. This can be prevented by removing all dead flower heads, or encouraged by leaving the flower heads on the plant.

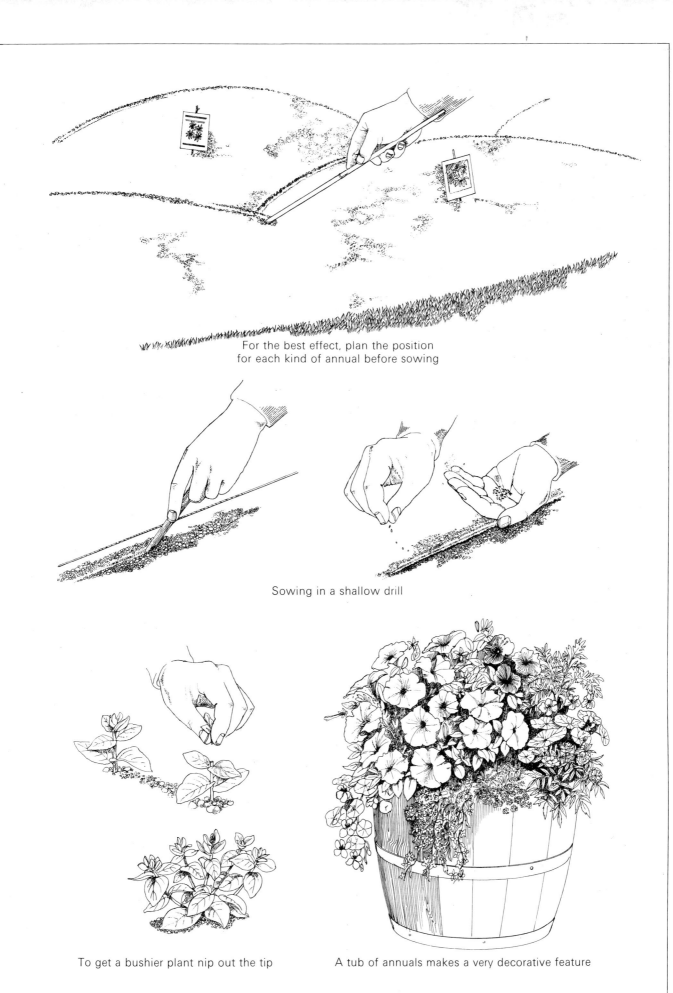

For the best effect, plan the position
for each kind of annual before sowing

Sowing in a shallow drill

To get a bushier plant nip out the tip   A tub of annuals makes a very decorative feature

Floss Flower

Ageratum

Site: sunny and sheltered

Soil: ordinary

Height: 15 to 45 cm (6 to 18 in)

Spread: 23 to 30 cm (9 to 12 in)

Type of plant: half-hardy annual

Flowers: fluffy, blue, pink or white

Flowering time: summer

Sowing time: spring (under glass, 13°C, 55°F), outdoors in frost-free climates

Planting time: early summer, when danger of frost is past

Planting distance: 23 cm (9 in)

Species cultivated: *A. houstonianum* is the species from which most varieties are derived; recommended varieties: 'Blue Mink' 23 cm (9 in), 'Tall Blue' 45 cm (18 in), 'Blue Chip' 23 cm (9 in), 'Summer Snow' white, 15 cm (6 in), 'North Sea' pinkish mauve, 20 cm (8 in)

Cultivation and uses: water plants well in dry weather – particularly in early stages after planting out. Can be grown in flower beds and borders (good as edging plants) or in pots and window-boxes outdoors

Hollyhock

Althaea

Site: sunny, not exposed to strong winds

Soil: deep and well drained, enrich with manure or compost

Height: 2 m (6 ft) and more

Spread: 60 to 120 cm (2 to 4 ft)

Type of plant: hardy perennial, usually grown as a biennial

Flowers: single trumpet-shaped or fully double flowers (photograph) with wavy-edged petals. White, cream, yellow, pink, mauve. Carried in tall spikes

Flowering time: summer

Sowing time: late spring (outdoors)

Planting time: transplant in summer to permanent site

Planting distance: 60 cm (2 ft)

Species cultivated: *A. rosea* is the species from which most varieties and colour forms are derived; treat as biennials (the plants will flower in the second summer after sowing)

Cultivation and uses: perennial but often best raised from seed each year to keep down rust disease; stake the flower spikes to avoid wind rock. Position as a focal point or against walls and by doors and windows. Traditional cottage garden plants

Love-lies-bleeding
Amaranthus

Site: sunny and sheltered

Soil: ordinary, moisture-retentive

Height: up to 1.25 m (4 ft)

Spread: 1 to 1.25 m (3 to 4 ft)

Type of plant: half-hardy annual

Flowers: red or pale green tassels up to 45 cm (18 in) long

Flowering time: midsummer to autumn

Sowing time: spring (under glass, 13°C, 55°F), early summer (outdoors) or early spring in frost-free climates

Planting time: early summer for plants raised under glass

Planting distance: 60 cm (2 ft)

Species cultivated: *A. caudatus* (photograph) has red tassels and its variety 'Viridis' pale green tassels; *A. tricolor* (Joseph's coat) has green leaves splashed with yellow and red making it a good foliage plant

Cultivation and uses: keep soil moist in dry weather can be grown in a container outdoors or in flower beds and borders. Flowers last well in water

Pimpernel
Anagallis

Site: sunny

Soil: light and well drained

Height: 15 cm (6 in)

Spread: 23 cm (9 in)

Type of plant: half-hardy annual

Flowers: rich blue, often with scarlet centre

Flowering time: summer

Sowing time: late spring where plants are to flower; thin to 30 cm (1 ft) when large enough to handle

Species cultivated: *A. arvensis caerulea* (photograph); *A. linifolia monelli*; both have rich blue flowers

Cultivation and uses: no special requirements, but do dislike waterlogged conditions; good edging plants for beds and borders

Snapdragon
Antirrhinum

Site: sunny

Soil: ordinary, well drained

Height: 20 to 100 cm (8 to 39 in)

Spread: 23 to 30 cm (9 to 12 in)

Type of plant: half-hardy annual

Flowers: white, yellow, pink, orange, yellow and mauve carried in short or long spikes

Flowering time: summer to autumn

Sowing time: spring (under glass, 15°C, 59°F) or outdoors in frost-free climates

Planting time: late spring to early summer

Planting distance: 23 to 30 cm (9 to 12 in)

Species cultivated: most varieties are derived from the perennial *A. majus* but are treated as annuals; recommended varieties: 'Butterfly Mixed' 75 cm (2½ ft), with double, more frilly flowers than normal, 'Coronette Mixed' 45 cm (18 in), 'Floral Carpet' 20 cm (8 in). There are many good single-coloured strains (photograph) which vary in height

Cultivation and uses: pinch plants when 8 cm (3 in) high; water when soil is very dry. Good plants for containers outdoors, for beds, borders and massed displays. Last well as cut flowers

African Daisy
Arctotis

Site: sunny and sheltered

Soil: light and well drained

Height: 60 cm (2 ft)

Spread: 45 cm (18 in)

Type of plant: half-hardy annual

Flowers: white, cream, yellow, orange, red and mauve 'daisies'

Flowering time: summer

Sowing time: early spring (under glass, 16°C, 60°F), outdoors in frost-free areas only

Planting time: early summer when danger of frost is past

Planting distance: 30 cm (1 ft)

Species cultivated: *A. grandis* has white flowers but mixed varieties (photograph) are offered in a wide range of colours

Cultivation and uses: no special requirements. Good plants for warm beds and borders. Flowers last well in water if picked before fully open

Begonia

Begonia

Site: sunny and sheltered

Soil: light but moisture-retentive

Height: 15 to 30 cm (6 to 12 in)

Spread: 15 to 30 cm (6 to 12 in)

Type of plant: half-hardy annual

Flowers: four-petalled with a central cluster of yellow stamens. White, pink, red or bi-coloured

Flowering time: summer

Sowing time: late winter or early spring (under glass, 21°C, 70°F), spring outdoors in frost-free climates

Planting time: early summer, when danger of frost is past

Planting distance: 23 cm (9 in)

Species cultivated: *B. semperflorens* is the parent of a wide range of varieties which are really perennial, though they are killed by frost and usually treated as annuals; recommended varieties: 'Indian Maid' red flowers, bronze foliage, 23 cm (9 in), 'Galaxy' mixed, 23 cm (9 in), 'Organdy' mixed, 23 cm (9 in), (photograph)

Cultivation and uses: water in dry weather; good for edging flower beds and borders and for massing together; suitable for window-boxes if kept well watered, can be potted up and overwintered in a greenhouse

Daisy

Bellis

Site: sunny or partially shady

Soil: ordinary

Height: 10 to 15 cm (4 to 6 in)

Spread: 15 cm (6 in)

Type of plant: hardy perennial

Flowers: white, pink or crimson double or semi-double

Flowering time: spring

Sowing time: late spring (under glass, 10°C, 50°F), early summer (outdoors)

Planting time: late summer

Planting distance: 23 cm (9 in)

Species cultivated: all varieties grown for spring bedding are derived from *B. perennis*. Giant Double Mixed, 15 cm (6 in), (photograph) and Pomponette Mixed, 10 cm (4 in), are particularly good

Cultivation and uses: no special requirements. Can be propagated by division after flowering or raised each year from seed and treated as an annual; good as an edging plant in beds and borders

Swan River Daisy

Brachycome

Site: sunny and sheltered

Soil: ordinary

Height: 30 cm (12 in)

Spread: 30 cm (12 in)

Type of plant: half-hardy annual

Flowers: white, pink, mauve, blue and purple 'daisies'

Flowering time: summer

Sowing time: spring (under glass, 15°C, 59°F), late spring (outdoors where plants are to flower)

Planting time: early summer for plants raised under glass. Thin out plants grown outdoors to 15 cm (6 in)

Planting distance: 15 cm (6 in)

Species cultivated: *B. iberidifolia* is sold in mixed colours (photograph)

Cultivation and uses: no special requirements. A good plant for the front of beds and borders; particularly effective when massed

Pearl Grass

Briza

Site: sunny

Soil: ordinary

Height: 45 cm (18 in)

Spread: 23 to 30 cm (9 to 12 in)

Type of plant: hardy annual

Flowers: greenish white pod-like flowers which are carried on wiry stems, gently arching at the tips

Flowering time: summer

Sowing time: spring, outdoors where plants are to flower. Thin to 15 cm (6 in) when plants are large enough to handle

Species cultivated: *B. maxima* is the annual variety grown (photograph)

Cultivation and uses: no special requirements. Pick flowers in late summer and dry for winter flower arrangements

Pot Marigold

Calendula

Site: sunny or partially shady

Soil: ordinary

Height: 30 to 60 cm (1 to 2 ft)

Spread: 30 to 60 cm (1 to 2 ft)

Type of plant: hardy annual

Flowers: large single, double or semi-double daisies in shades of cream, orange and yellow

Flowering time: summer

Sowing time: spring, outdoors where plants are to flower; thin to 30 cm (12 in) when plants are large enough to handle

Species cultivated: *C. officinalis* is the species from which the many varieties have been derived. Recommended varieties: 'Fiesta Gitana' 30 cm (12 in), double, mixed, 'Radio' 45 cm (18 in), double, bright orange, 'Orange King' (photograph) 45 cm (18 in), double, orange, 'Golden King' 45 cm (18 in), double, bright yellow

Cultivation and uses: no special requirements. Plants will seed themselves profusely but seedlings usually show a deterioration in flower size and quality. Good plants for the front of a border. Flowers last well in water

China Aster

Callistephus

Site: sunny or partially shady

Soil: ordinary but fertile

Height: 23 to 60 cm (9 to 24 in)

Spread: 30 cm (12 in)

Type of plant: half-hardy annual

Flowers: single, double and semi-double 'daisies' in shades of red, pink, mauve, purple and white

Flowering time: summer

Sowing time: spring (under glass, 15°C, 59°F), outdoors in frost-free climates

Planting time: early summer

Planting distance: 23 cm (9 in)

Species cultivated: *C. chinensis* is the parent of many mixed varieties and also of a range of single-coloured strains

Cultivation and uses: water well in dry weather. Good plants for the front of beds and borders

Bellflower

Campanula

Site: sunny or partially shady

Soil: ordinary, well drained

Height: 60 to 120 cm (2 to 4 ft)

Spread: 30 to 60 cm (1 to 2 ft)

Type of plant: hardy biennials and perennials

Flowers: large blue or white bells

Flowering time: early to late summer

Sowing time: early to late spring (under glass, 10°C, 50°F), late spring or early summer (outdoors)

Planting time: summer

Planting distance: 45 cm (18 in)

Species cultivated: both *C. persicifolia*, (photograph) and *C. pyramidalis* (chimney bellflower, steeple bells) can be grown in the same way; the first is a true perennial which will increase in size as well as sowing its own seed; the second is a short-lived perennial best treated as a biennial; both flower in the second summer after sowing. *C. pyramidalis* is available in white or blue varieties, *C. persicifolia* as a mixture of the two colours

Cultivation and uses: *C. pyramidalis* may need staking in exposed gardens. Cut down to ground level in winter. Flowers of *C. persicifolia* last well in water and *C. pyramidalis* will grow well in pots

Cupid's Dart

Catananche

Site: sunny, sheltered

Soil: ordinary, well drained

Height: 60 cm (2 ft)

Spread: 30 cm (1 ft)

Type of plant: hardy perennial

Flowers: lavender-blue or white 'daisies' carried on wiry stems

Flowering time: summer

Sowing time: early spring (under glass, 13°C, 55°F), late spring (outdoors)

Planting time: early summer (for plants raised under glass); those sown outdoors should be thinned when large enough to handle to leave one every 23 cm (9 in)

Planting distance: 23 cm (9 in)

Species cultivated: *C. caerulea* (blue cupidone) is available in blue (photograph) and white varieties

Cultivation and uses: although a perennial this plant has a tendency to be short lived and may have to be renewed from seed frequently. Cut down to ground level in winter. A good plant for sunny beds and borders. Flowers can be dried, for the silvery calyx on each bloom is 'everlasting'

Prince of Wales' Feather
Celosia

Site: sunny and sheltered

Soil: ordinary, well drained

Height: 25 to 45 cm (10 to 18 in)

Spread: 15 to 23 cm (6 to 9 in)

Type of plant: half-hardy annual

Flowers: red, yellow or orange plumes or similarly coloured 'combs'

Flowering time: summer

Sowing time: late winter or early spring (under glass, 21°C, 70°F), outdoors in frost-free climates only

Planting time: summer, when danger of frost is past

Planting distance: 30 cm (1 ft)

Species cultivated: *C. argentea pyramidalis* (photograph) is the plumed kind, *C. argentea cristata* has dense, wavy 'comb'-like flowerheads which have resulted in it being given the name 'Cockscomb'; both have compact or taller growing varieties

Cultivation and uses: after pricking out and growing on, pot the seedlings up into 9-cm (3½-in) pots; they will then make sturdy plants before being planted out; they can also be grown as greenhouse pot plants

Cornflower, Sweet Sultan
Centaurea

Site: sunny

Soil: ordinary, well drained

Height: 30 to 90 cm (1 to 3 ft)

Spread: 30 to 60 cm (1 to 2 ft)

Type of plant: hardy annual

Flowers: fluffy round flowers in shades of blue, pink, mauve, red, purple and white

Flowering time: summer

Sowing time: spring (outdoors) where plants are to flower. Thin seedlings to 23 or 30 cm (9 or 12 in) when large enough to handle

Species cultivated: *C. cyanus* is the common annual cornflower or bluebottle; recommended varieties of this species are: Tall Double Mixed, 90 cm (3 ft), 'Blue Diadem' 60 cm (2 ft), large double flowers, Polka Dot Mixed 45 cm (18 in); there are dwarf mixed strains only 30 cm (1 ft) high; *C. moschata* (sweet sultan) (photograph) has fringed fragrant flowers; the variety Giant Mixed, 60 cm (2 ft), is recommended

Cultivation and uses: stake taller varieties with twiggy branches; good in annual borders. Flowers last well in water

Valerian

Centranthus

Site: sunny

Soil: light, well drained

Height: 60 cm (2 ft)

Spread: 60 cm (2 ft)

Type of plant: hardy annual

Flowers: usually deep pink, but a white variety is available. Small flowers are carried in rounded clusters

Flowering time: early to late summer

Sowing time: late spring to early summer (outdoors)

Planting time: move plants to permanent site in autumn; (can also be sown where they are to flower and later thinned)

Planting distance: 30 cm (1 ft)

Species cultivated: *C. macrosiphon* (photograph) is the annual species most commonly grown; its variety 'Albus' has white flowers

Cultivation and uses: plants raised from seed will flower in the second summer after sowing; cut down to ground level in winter. An excellent plant for hot, dry soils and for planting in walls. See also page 91 for perennial kinds

Wallflower

Cheiranthus

Site: sunny

Soil: ordinary, well drained

Height: 23 to 45 cm (9 to 18 in)

Spread: 30 to 45 cm (12 to 18 in)

Type of plant: hardy biennial

Flowers: scented, orange, yellow, pink, cream, crimson and mauve, often streaked

Flowering time: spring to early summer

Sowing time: late spring (outdoors)

Planting time: transplant seedlings into rows during summer, spacing them 15 cm (6 in) apart; move to flowering position in late summer, early autumn. Snap off base of taproot when planting

Planting distance: 23 cm (9 in)

Species cultivated: *C. cheiri* is the species from which the popular spring-flowering varieties have been derived; recommended varieties: 'Blood Red' 45 cm (18 in), crimson, 'Cloth of Gold' 45 cm (18 in), yellow; also many mixed varieties (photograph)

Cultivation and uses: perennials but best treated as biennials and raised afresh from seed each year. Add a little lime to the soil if it is at all acid; excellent spring bedding plants; can be interplanted with bulbs; may also be grown in walls

Chrysanthemum

Chrysanthemum

Site: sunny

Soil: ordinary, well drained

Height: 75 cm (2½ ft)

Spread: 30 cm (1 ft)

Type of plant: hardy annual

Flowers: large daisies in shades of yellow, red, orange and white, usually with contrastingly coloured zones

Flowering time: summer

Sowing time: spring (outdoors where plants are to flower); thin seedlings when large enough to handle leaving one every 23 cm (9 in)

Species cultivated: *C. carinatum* is the most popular annual species of which mixed varieties are available (photograph)

Cultivation and uses: no special requirements, though in exposed situations the plants may need staking with twiggy branches. Good in annual bedding schemes, especially if planted in large groups

Spider Flower

Cleome

Site: sunny or partially shady

Soil: light and well drained but fertile

Height: 1 m (3 ft)

Spread: 60 cm (2 ft)

Type of plant: half-hardy annual

Flowers: pink or white with long stamens which give them the 'spidery' appearance. Carried in large round heads

Flowering time: summer

Sowing time: early spring (under glass, 15°C, 59°F), outdoors in frost-free climates only

Planting time: early summer, when danger of frost is past

Planting distance: 30 to 45 cm (1 to 2 ft)

Species cultivated: *C. spinosa* (syn. *C. pungens*) is available in mixed varieties such as 'Colour Fountain' and in single colours such as 'Pink Queen' (photograph)

Cultivation and uses: pinch out young plants when 10 cm (4 in) high to encourage bushiness. Good plants for filling sunny gaps in beds and borders. Can also be grown as pot plants outdoors or in a cool greenhouse

Tickseed

Coreopsis (or Calliopsis)

Site: sunny

Soil: light, well drained

Height: 30 to 90 cm (1 to 3 ft)

Spread: 30 to 60 cm (1 to 2 ft)

Type of plant: hardy annual

Flowers: yellow, mauve or crimson 'daisies' with a conspicuous central boss

Flowering time: summer

Sowing time: early spring (under glass, 13°C, 55°F), late spring (outdoors where plants are to flower)

Planting time: early summer, for plants raised under glass; thin those raised outdoors when large enough to handle

Planting distance: 23 cm (9 in)

Species cultivated: *C. tinctoria* and *C. drummondii* have both given rise to some good varieties. 'Golden Crown' (photograph), 60 cm (2 ft), is yellow with a dark brown centre, 'Dwarf Dazzler' 30 cm (12 in), is crimson edged with gold. Mixed varieties are also available

Cultivation and uses: no special requirements; good plants for massing together in beds and borders

Cosmea

Cosmos

Site: sunny, sheltered

Soil: ordinary

Height: 60 to 90 cm (2 to 3 ft)

Spread: 45 cm (18 in)

Type of plant: half-hardy annual

Flowers: large petalled, in shades of red, pink, mauve and white. Double varieties are also available

Flowering time: summer

Sowing time: early spring (under glass, 13°C, 55°F), late spring (outdoors where plants are to flower)

Planting time: early summer, for plants raised under glass; thin out plants grown outdoors to 23 cm (9 in)

Planting distance: 23 cm (9 in)

Species cultivated: *C. bipinnatus* is available in mixed and single-coloured varieties. The double variety 'Bright Lights' is mixed, relatively early flowering and grows to a height of 60 cm (2 ft)

Cultivation and uses: no special requirements; good plants for massing in flower borders; flowers last well in water

Cigar Flower
Cuphea

Site: sunny, sheltered

Soil: ordinary, well drained

Height: 30 cm (1 ft)

Spread: 30 cm (1 ft)

Type of plant: half-hardy annual

Flowers: small red tubular flowers tipped with deep purple

Flowering time: spring to autumn

Sowing time: spring (under glass, 15°C, 59°F) or outdoors in frost-free climates

Planting time: early summer, when danger of frost is past

Planting distance: 30 cm (1 ft)

Species cultivated: *C. ignea* (photograph) and *C. miniata* are the two species most commonly grown; 'Firefly' is a good variety of *C. miniata*

Cultivation and uses: no special requirements. Good plants for sunny beds and borders; also frequently grown as cool greenhouse pot plants

Larkspur
Delphinium

Site: sunny

Soil: ordinary, not too dry

Height: 30 to 120 cm (1 to 4 ft)

Spread: 30 cm (1 ft)

Type of plant: hardy annual

Flowers: tall spikes of white, pink, mauve, blue or purple blooms

Flowering time: summer

Sowing time: spring (outdoors where plants are to flower; thin seedlings to 23 cm (9 in) when large enough to handle

Species cultivated: *D. ajacis* is the parent of most annual varieties of larkspur; recommended varieties: 'White Spire' 120 cm (4 ft), (photograph), 'Blue Spire' 120 cm (4 ft), 'Hyacinth Flowered' 45 cm (18 in), mixed, relatively early flowering; many mixed varieties are available and these vary in height

Cultivation and uses: stake taller varieties with twiggy branches; good plants for beds and borders where they can be positioned towards the back to give height to a display

Annual Pink
Dianthus

Site: sunny

Soil: ordinary, well drained

Height: 15 to 30 cm (6 to 12 in)

Spread: 23 to 30 cm (9 to 12 in)

Type of plant: half-hardy annual

Flowers: single or double flowers in shades of red, mauve, pink and white

Flowering time: summer

Sowing time: late winter to early spring (under glass, 15°C, 59°F), outdoors in frost-free climates

Planting time: early summer, when danger of frost is past

Planting distance: 15 to 23 cm (6 to 9 in)

Species cultivated: *D. chinensis* and its variety *heddewigii* are available in a number of brilliantly coloured varieties; among the best of these are: 'Queen of Hearts' 30 cm (12 in), single, red, 'Baby Doll Mixed' 15 cm (6 in), 'Magic Charms' 15 cm (6 in), single, fringed, mixed, 'Brilliancy' (photograph) single, rich cerise-pink, 'Snowflake' 20 cm (8 in), single white

Cultivation and uses: no special requirements; excellent plants for the front of a sunny border, or for planting in pockets on the rock garden; look particularly at home planted alongside paths

Sweet William
Dianthus

Site: sunny or partially shady

Soil: ordinary, fertile

Height: 15 to 45 cm (6 to 18 in)

Spread: 30 cm (12 in)

Type of plant: hardy biennial

Flowers: pink, mauve or white, most having contrasting zones; scented

Flowering time: late spring to summer

Sowing time: early summer (outdoors)

Planting time: transplant seedlings into rows during summer, spacing them 15 cm (6 in) apart. Move to flowering position in late summer

Planting distance: 23 to 30 cm (9 to 12 in)

Species cultivated: *D. barbatus* is the species from which all our present-day varieties of Sweet William have been derived; recommended varieties: 'Auricula-Eyed Mixed' (photograph) 45 cm (18 in), all with white eyes, 'Indian Carpet' 15 cm (6 in), mixed, 'Double Mixed' 45 cm (18 in), with double flowers. Single-coloured varieties are also available

Cultivation and uses: superb plants for an early summer display; plant in beds and borders. Flowers last well in water

Foxglove
Digitalis

Site: partial to heavy shade

Soil: fertile and moisture-retentive

Height: 90 to 150 cm (3 to 5 ft)

Spread: 30 to 60 cm (1 to 2 ft)

Type of plant: hardy biennial

Flowers: tall spikes of bell-like flowers in shades of pink, mauve, pale yellow and white with dark spots in their throats

Flowering time: late spring to midsummer

Sowing time: late spring (outdoors)

Planting time: transplant seedlings during summer, spacing them 15 cm (6 in) apart; move to flowering position in late summer and early autumn

Planting distance: 30 cm (1 ft)

Species cultivated: *D. purpurea* is the biennial kind which is raised each year from seeds and from which several strains have been derived; recommended varieties: Excelsior Hybrids, 1.5 m (5 ft), mixed, 'Foxy' 1 m, (3 ft), mixed; single-coloured varieties are also available (photograph)

Cultivation and uses: taller varieties may need staking in exposed gardens; superb plants for woodland and wild gardens. Many seed themselves quite freely

Star of the Veldt
Dimorphotheca

Site: sunny

Soil: ordinary, well drained

Height: 15 to 30 cm (6 to 12 in)

Spread: 30 cm (1 ft)

Type of plant: hardy annual

Flowers: large 'daisies' in shades of yellow, orange, cream and white, all with a dark central boss

Flowering time: summer

Sowing time: late spring (outdoors where plants are to flower); thin when large enough to handle to leave one plant every 23 cm (9 in)

Species cultivated: *D. sinuata* (syn. *D. aurantiaca*) (photograph) is the species from which most annual varieties have been derived; recommended varieties: Aurantiaca Hybrids 30 cm (1 ft), mixed, 'Glistening White' 23 cm (9 in), 'Orange Glory' 30 cm (1 ft), large flowers of brilliant orange

Cultivation and uses: no special requirements; good in beds and borders and alongside paths; flowers last well in water

Teasel

Dipsacus

Site: sunny

Soil: ordinary

Height: 120 to 180 cm (4 to 6 ft)

Spread: 60 to 90 cm (2 to 3 ft)

Type of plant: hardy biennial

Flowers: large green spiky heads which carry small lilac purple flowers

Flowering time: early to late summer

Sowing time: early summer (outdoors where the plants are to flower); thin seedlings to 30 cm (1 ft) when plants are large enough to handle

Species cultivated: *D. fullonum* (Fuller's teasel) (photograph) is the kind most widely grown; it will flower in the year following sowing and will seed itself quite freely

Cultivation and uses: no particular requirements. Good plant for wild and woodland gardens. Cut the flower heads in late summer and dry them for winter decoration – may be sprayed with gold or silver paint. Originally used to tease wool

Californian Poppy

Eschscholzia

Site: sunny

Soil: ordinary, well drained

Height: 15 to 30 cm (6 to 12 in)

Spread: 15 to 30 cm (6 to 12 in)

Type of plant: hardy annual

Flowers: poppy-like blooms in shades of red, orange, yellow, cream and white

Flowering time: summer

Sowing time: late spring (outdoors where plants are to flower); thin seedlings when large enough to handle to leave one every 15 cm (6 in)

Species cultivated: *E. californica* is the species from which the wide range of annual varieties has been derived; recommended varieties: Single Mixed (photograph) 30 cm (1 ft), 'Ballerina' 30 cm (1 ft), double mixed, 'Miniature Primrose' 15 cm (6 in), pale yellow

Cultivation and uses: no special requirements. Good in annual borders; 'Miniature Primrose' can be sown in pockets on the rock garden. Can be grown in containers

Treasure Flower

Gazania

Site: sunny, sheltered

Soil: ordinary, well drained

Height: 30 cm (12 in)

Spread: 30 cm (12 in)

Type of plant: half-hardy annual

Flowers: large, brightly coloured daisies in shades of red, orange, pink and yellow; many are bi-coloured

Flowering time: summer to autumn

Sowing time: early spring (under glass, 15°C, 59°F), outdoors in frost-free climates

Planting time: late spring, when danger of frost is past

Planting distance: 23 cm (9 in)

Species cultivated: most varieties grown are hybrids of *G. splendens* (photograph) and are in mixed colours

Cultivation and uses: the plants are really perennials but will only survive the winter in frost-free climates; for that reason they are usually treated as half-hardy annuals and raised afresh each year from seeds. Excellent at the front of beds and borders, in walls, containers and pockets in the rock garden

Godetia

Godetia

Site: sunny or partially shady

Soil: ordinary, well drained

Height: 23 to 60 cm (9 to 24 in)

Spread: 23 to 30 cm (9 to 12 in)

Type of plant: hardy annual

Flowers: large, thin-petalled blooms in shades of red, pink, mauve and white; many are bi-coloured and there are several double varieties

Flowering time: summer to autumn

Sowing time: spring (outdoors where plants are to flower); thin to leave one plant every 15 cm (6 in) when seedlings are large enough to handle

Species cultivated: most varieties are derived from *G. grandiflora* and *G. amoena*; recommended varieties: Tall Double Mixed 60 cm (2 ft), Azalea-Flowered Mixed 45 cm (18 in), double, 'Sybil Sherwood' 30 cm (12 in), pale pink and white, 'Kelvedon Glory' 45 cm (18 in), salmon, Dwarf Bedding Mixed 23 cm (9 in)

Cultivation and uses: water well in dry weather; good plants for beds and borders and for growing in containers provided that the soil is not allowed to dry out

Baby's Breath

Gypsophila

Site: sunny

Soil: ordinary, well drained; dress with lime if acid

Height: 45 cm (18 in)

Spread: 45 cm (18 in)

Type of plant: hardy annual

Flowers: delicate open blooms of white or pink

Flowering time: summer

Sowing time: spring (outdoors where plants are to flower); thin seedlings when large enough to handle leaving one every 15 cm (6 in)

Species cultivated: *G. elegans* is available in both white-flowered (photograph) and pink-flowered varieties

Cultivation and uses: no special requirements. Good plant for beds and borders, especially where other annuals are being grown. Flower sprays last well in water

Sunflower

Helianthus

Site: sunny and sheltered

Soil: ordinary

Height: 60 to 300 cm (2 to 10 ft) and more

Spread: 60 to 90 cm (2 to 3 ft)

Type of plant: hardy annual

Flowers: yellow, red or orange 'daisies', usually with large black centres, some are double

Flowering time: summer to autumn

Sowing time: spring (outdoors where plants are to flower); sow seeds in groups of two at 30 cm (1 ft) stations and thin out after germination; tall varieties should have a final spacing of 60 cm (2 ft), lower-growing varieties a spacing of 30 cm (1 ft)

Species cultivated: the annual kinds are derived mainly from *H. annuus* (photograph); recommended varieties: 'Sunburst' 120 cm (4 ft), red, yellow and orange flowers with contrasting markings, 'Dwarf Double Sungold' 60 cm (2 ft), double, bright yellow, 'Tall Single' 240 cm (8 ft) and more, yellow flowers of good size

Cultivation and uses: stake tall varieties to prevent wind rock; good plants for the back of a border or against a house wall; great fun for children to grow

Straw Flower

Helichrysum

Site: sunny

Soil: ordinary

Height: 30 to 90 cm (1 to 3 ft)

Spread: 30 cm (1 ft)

Type of plant: hardy annual

Flowers: double 'everlasting' blooms in shades of yellow, orange, red, pink, cream and white

Flowering time: summer to autumn

Sowing time: spring (outdoors where plants are to flower); thin seedlings to 23 cm (9 in) when large enough to handle

Species cultivated: *H. bracteatum monstrosum* (photograph) is the species from which the annual varieties have been derived; recommended varieties: Tall Large Flowered Mixed 1 m (3 ft), 'Bright Bikini' 30 cm (1 ft), mixed, 'Hot Bikini' 30 cm (1 ft), bright red

Cultivation and uses: stake taller varieties with twiggy branches in exposed gardens; good plants for annual borders. Gather when flowers are fully open and dry for winter decoration – dried flowers retain their colour exceptionally well

Heliotrope, Cherry Pie

Heliotropium

Site: sunny

Soil: ordinary

Height: 45 to 75 cm (18 to 30 in)

Spread: 30 to 60 cm (1 to 2 ft)

Type of plant: half-hardy annual

Flowers: dense heads of small violet-purple or pale blue blooms; very fragrant

Flowering time: summer to autumn

Sowing time: early spring (under glass, 15°C, 59°F), outdoors in frost-free climates only

Planting time: early summer when danger of frost is past

Planting distance: 30 cm (1 ft)

Species cultivated: *H. peruvianum* (cherry pie) is the parent of the varieties grown for summer bedding; recommended varieties: 'Marine' (photograph) 60 cm (2 ft), violet blue; mixed varieties which vary in height are also available

Cultivation and uses: this plant is really a half-hardy perennial which is usually grown as a half-hardy annual. Taller specimens can be raised if the plants are grown for two years, being given winter protection under glass. It can also be made to flower in winter under glass. Outdoors it can be grown in beds and borders as well as in containers. Plants grown as standards should be staked

Immortelle

Helipterum (syn. Acroclinium and Rhodanthe)

Site: sunny

Soil: ordinary, well drained

Height: 30 to 60 cm (1 to 2 ft)

Spread: 30 cm (1 ft)

Type of plant: hardy annual

Flowers: double and semi-double pink or white 'everlasting' blooms

Flowering time: summer

Sowing time: late spring (outdoors where plants are to flower); thin seedlings to 15 cm (6 in) when large enough to handle

Species cultivated: the most popular species for summer bedding is *H. roseum* (photograph), 60 cm (2 ft), which is usually sold in mixed varieties; *H. manglesii*, 30 cm (1 ft), is also freely available in pink or white shades

Cultivation and uses: no special requirements. Excellent in annual beds and borders; gather when flowers are fully open and dry for winter decoration. Dried flowers retain their colour well

Candytuft

Iberis

Site: sunny

Soil: ordinary

Height: 15 to 30 cm (6 to 12 in)

Spread: 30 cm (12 in)

Type of plant: hardy annual

Flowers: large heads of white, pink, mauve and crimson

Flowering time: summer

Sowing time: spring (outdoors where plants are to flower); thin to 15 cm (6 in) when seedlings are large enough to handle

Species cultivated: *I. amara* is the species from which the annual candytuft varieties are derived; recommended varieties: 'Fairy Mixed' 15 to 23 cm (6 to 9 in), 'Red Flash' 30 cm (1 ft), crimson, 'Hyacinth-flowered White' 30 cm (1 ft), fuller flower heads

Cultivation and uses: no special requirements; good plants for the front of beds and borders or for pockets in the rock garden

Burning Bush
Kochia

Site: sunny

Soil: ordinary

Height: 60 to 90 cm (2 to 3 ft)

Spread: 30 cm (12 in)

Type of plant: half-hardy annual

Flowers: unremarkable; the plant is grown for its mound of narrow leaves which are bright green in summer turning to crimson in autumn

Sowing time: spring (under glass, 15°C, 59°F), outdoors in frost-free climates only

Planting time: early summer, when danger of frost is past

Planting distance: 60 cm (2 ft)

Species cultivated: *K. scoparia trichophylla* (photograph), known variously as burning bush and summer cypress, is the best kind

Cultivation and uses: no special requirements. Best used as 'dot' plants among lower-growing summer bedding plants; suitable for growing in containers outdoors

Lantana
Lantana

Site: sunny

Soil: ordinary, well drained

Height: 3 m (10 ft) if allowed to grow unrestricted. More usually 30 to 60 cm (1 to 2 ft) if renewed each year from seeds or cuttings

Spread: 30 to 60 cm (1 to 2 ft) on year-old plants

Type of plant: half-hardy perennial

Flowers: flat heads of yellow to orange blooms

Flowering time: summer to autumn

Sowing time: spring (under glass, 15°C, 59°F), outdoors in frost-free climates

Planting time: early summer, when danger of frost is past

Planting distance: 60 cm (2 ft)

Species cultivated: *L. camara* (photograph) is the species most commonly grown

Cultivation and uses: pinch out the tips of young plants to encourage bushiness. Raise afresh each year or pot up the plants before autumn frosts and give winter protection; lantana is really a perennial and will last for many years in a container or grown outdoors in warm climates. Suitable also as a summer bedding plant and as a greenhouse pot plant

Sweet Pea

Lathyrus

Site: sunny

Soil: ordinary, fertile

Height: 60 to 180 cm (2 to 6 ft) depending on support

Spread: dependent upon kind of support; low-growing kinds 30 to 60 cm (1 to 2 ft)

Type of plant: hardy annual

Flowers: shades of red, pink, mauve, purple, blue, creamy yellow and white; most are scented

Flowering time: summer to autumn

Sowing time: late winter (under glass, 15°C, 59°F) spring (outdoors). For earliest flowers sow under glass in late autumn and overwinter in a cold frame

Planting time: late spring (if raised under glass)

Planting distance: 30 cm (1 ft), plant at foot of tripod or row of canes; support dwarf types with twiggy branches pushed into soil

Species cultivated: annual sweet peas are varieties of *L. odoratus*; recommended varieties: Spencer varieties, single and mixed colours (photograph), Jet Set Mixed, 1 m (3 ft), 'Knee-Hi' 60 cm (2 ft) if sown in spring, 120 cm (4 ft) if sown in autumn

Cultivation and uses: sow seeds in pots; pinch out tips when 8 cm (3 in) high; enrich ground with manure before planting. Feed regularly; remove faded flowers. Flowers last well in water

Tree Mallow

Lavatera

Site: sunny

Soil: ordinary

Height: 60 to 120 cm (2 to 4 ft)

Spread: 60 cm (2 ft)

Type of plant: hardy annual

Flowers: large trumpets of rich pink

Flowering time: summer to early autumn

Sowing time: late spring (outdoors where plants are to flower); thin seedlings to 45 cm (18 in) when large enough to handle

Species cultivated: *L. trimestris* (photograph) is the best annual kind and it is available in several good varieties: 'Loveliness' 60 cm (2 ft), 'Tanagra' 1 to 1.25 m (3 to 4 ft), more upright, 'Silver Cup' 60 cm (2 ft)

Cultivation and uses: no special requirements; plants may be used to form an annual hedge; look well in annual and mixed borders

Tidy Tips
Layia

Site: sunny

Soil: ordinary

Height: 30 cm (12 in)

Spread: 23 cm (9 in)

Type of plant: hardy annual

Flowers: delicate 'daisies' whose petals are yellow tipped with white

Flowering time: summer

Sowing time: spring (outdoors where plants are to flower); thin seedlings to 23 cm (9 in) when large enough to handle

Species cultivated: *L. elegans* (photograph) is the species most widely available

Cultivation and uses: no special requirements; good edging plant for beds and borders and for planting alongside paths

Thinning out seedlings

Stardust
Leptosiphon

Site: sunny

Soil: ordinary, well drained

Height: 15 cm (6 in)

Spread: 15 to 23 cm (6 to 9 in)

Type of plant: hardy annual

Flowers: tiny blooms of yellow, orange, pink, cream and red

Flowering time: summer

Sowing time: spring (outdoors where plants are to flower); thin seedlings to 8 or 10 cm (3 or 4 in) when large enough to handle

Species cultivated: *L. hybridus* (occasionally listed more correctly as *Gilia hybrida*) is available in mixed strains (photograph)

Cultivation and uses: excellent little plants for planting in pockets in the rock garden, between paving stones and alongside paths; good for the front of sunny beds and borders

Toadflax

Linaria

Site: sunny

Soil: ordinary

Height: 23 to 30 cm (9 to 12 in)

Spread: 15 cm (6 in)

Type of plant: hardy annual

Flowers: miniature snapdragons of pink, red, yellow, purple, cerise, orange and white (most flowers are bi-coloured)

Flowering time: summer and autumn

Sowing time: spring (outdoors where the plants are to flower); thin seedlings to 15 cm (6 in) when large enough to handle; can also be sown outdoors in autumn

Species cultivated: most annual varieties are derived from *L. maroccana* (photograph); recommended varieties: 'Fairy Bouquet' 23 cm (9 in), mixed, Excelsior Hybrids 30 cm (12 in), mixed

Cultivation and uses: when the first flowers fade, lightly clip the plants and they will bloom again later in the summer. Good plants for the front of beds and borders and for planting in pockets in the rock garden

Lobelia

Lobelia

Site: sunny or partially shady

Soil: ordinary

Height: 10 to 15 cm (4 to 6 in)

Spread: 30 cm (12 in)

Type of plant: half-hardy annual

Flowers: small white, pink, blue, carmine or purple blooms

Flowering time: summer to autumn

Sowing time: early spring (under glass, 15°C, 59°F), outdoors in frost-free climates only

Planting time: early summer

Planting distance: 15 cm (6 in)

Species cultivated: most of the annual varieties have been derived from *L. erinus* and *L. tenuior*; (the photograph shows a mixed variety of *L. erinus*); recommended varieties: 'Cambridge Blue' pale blue, 'Crystal Palace' dark blue, 'Red Cascade' magenta, trailing, 'White Lady', 'Sapphire', deep blue, trailing

Cultivation and uses: plant out in clumps for seedlings are too small to separate. Excellent edging plants, often alternated with alyssum; do well in containers and hanging baskets (particularly trailing varieties); although a tender perennial, the plant is almost always treated as a half-hardy annual, being raised afresh from seed each year

Sweet Alyssum
Lobularia

Site: sunny

Soil: ordinary

Height: 8 to 10 cm (3 to 4 in)

Spread: up to 30 cm (12 in)

Type of plant: hardy annual

Flowers: sweet-smelling domes of pink, lilac or white blooms are held over small mounds of foliage

Flowering time: summer to autumn

Sowing time: spring (outdoors where the plants are to flower); thin the seedlings to 10 cm (4 in) when large enough to handle

Species cultivated: *L. maritima* is the parent of a wide range of different coloured varieties; recommended varieties: 'Little Dorrit', white, 'Rosie O'Day' pink (photograph), 'Wonderland' rich reddish pink, 'Royal Carpet' purple, 'Snowdrift' white

Cultivation and uses: no special requirements. Good edging plant for beds and borders, often alternated with lobelia; also excellent in pockets in the rock garden, gaps in paving and on walls

Honesty
Lunaria

Site: sunny or shady

Soil: ordinary

Height: 60 to 90 cm (2 to 3 ft)

Spread: 30 cm (1 ft)

Type of plant: hardy biennial

Flowers: four-petalled magenta flowers are followed by oval, shiny cream seed cases

Flowering time: spring to early summer

Sowing time: late spring (outdoors where the plants are to flower); thin the seedlings to 23 cm (9 in) when large enough to handle

Species cultivated: *L. annua* (syn. *L. biennis*) (photograph) is the biennial kind; it has a white-flowered variety, *alba*, and one with variegated leaves, *variegata*, both of which come true from seed

Cultivation and uses: the plants will seed themselves prolifically. Good plants for shady spots under trees and for sowing in drifts in beds and borders. The stems of papery seed cases can be dried for winter decoration

Brompton Stock

Matthiola

Site: sunny

Soil: fertile, well drained

Height: 45 cm (18 in)

Spread: 23 cm (9 in)

Type of plant: hardy biennial

Flowers: tall columns of scented blooms coloured white, pink, crimson, mauve or purple

Flowering time: spring

Sowing time: early summer (in cold frame)

Planting time: autumn, or spring (overwinter in frame)

Planting distance: 30 cm (1 ft)

Species cultivated: the Brompton stock is *M. incana* which is usually sold in single colours (photograph) or as a mixed variety

Cultivation and uses: no special requirements. Superbly scented spring bedding plants which look well in beds, borders and containers

Livingstone Daisy

Mesembryanthemum

Site: sunny

Soil: ordinary, well drained

Height: 8 cm (3 in)

Spread: 30 cm (1 ft)

Type of plant: half-hardy annual

Flowers: large daisies in vibrant shades of pink, red, orange, magenta, yellow and white, often bi-coloured

Flowering time: summer

Sowing time: early spring (under glass, 15°C, 59°F), outdoors in frost-free climates only

Planting time: early summer, when danger of frost is past

Planting distance: 15 cm (6 in)

Species cultivated: *M. criniflorum* (syn. *Dorotheanthus bellidiformis*) is usually sold in mixed varieties (photograph)

Cultivation and uses: this plant really does appreciate sun and its flowers close up in shade; an excellent subject for the front of beds and borders and for planting on walls and in rock garden pockets

Bells of Ireland
Moluccella

Site: sunny and sheltered

Soil: ordinary, well drained

Height: 90 cm (3 ft)

Spread: 30 cm (1 ft)

Type of plant: half-hardy annual

Flowers: small, insignificant white blooms backed by conspicuous green cup-shaped calyces

Flowering time: summer

Sowing time: early spring (under glass, 15°C, 59°F), outdoors in frost-free climates only

Planting time: early summer

Planting distance: 30 cm (1 ft)

Species cultivated: *M. laevis* (photograph) is the kind most widely grown

Cultivation and uses: no special requirements; good plants for arranging in drifts in beds and borders. The flower spikes can be dried for winter decoration

Forget-me-not
Myosotis

Site: sunny or partially shady

Soil: ordinary

Height: 15 to 30 cm (6 to 12 in)

Spread: 15 to 30 cm (6 to 12 in)

Type of plant: hardy biennial

Flowers: small pink, pale blue, dark blue or white blooms carried in short arching sprays

Flowering time: spring

Sowing time: early summer (outdoors where the plants are to flower). Thin seedlings to 10 or 15 cm (4 or 6 in) when large enough to handle

Species cultivated: varieties of *M. sylvatica* are the ones grown for spring bedding; recommended varieties: 'Blue Ball' 15 cm (6 in), bright blue, 'Ultramarine' 15 cm (6 in), deep blue, 'Blue Bouquet' 30 cm (12 in), bright blue, 'Alba' 23 cm (9 in), white, 'Carmine King' 23 cm (9 in), rich pink

Cultivation and uses: plants will seed themselves freely in successive years, excellent for naturalising under trees and for using as ground cover among spring-bedding plants such as wallflowers and tulips

Nemesia

Nemesia

Site: sunny

Soil: ordinary, fertile

Height: 23 to 30 cm (9 to 12 in)

Spread: 15 to 23 cm (6 to 9 in)

Type of plant: half-hardy annual

Flowers: small, trumpet-shaped blooms in shades of orange, yellow, pink, red, cerise, pale blue, lilac and white

Flowering time: summer

Sowing time: spring (under glass, 15°C, 59°F), outdoors in frost-free climates only

Planting time: early summer, when danger of frost is past

Planting distance: 20 cm (8 in)

Species cultivated: the varieties available are derived from *N. strumosa* and *N. versicolor* (the blue and lilac shades coming from *N. versicolor*). Recommended varieties: 'Carnival' 30 cm (12 in) (photograph), all shades except the blues, 'Blue Gem' 23 cm (9 in), pale blue, 'Dwarf Gem' 23 cm (9 in), mixed, including blues

Cultivation and uses: try to prevent the soil around the plants from becoming excessively dry. Can be grown as pot plants in a cool greenhouse. Good plants for summer bedding; particularly effective when massed

Baby Blue-eyes

Nemophila

Site: sunny or partially shady and cool

Soil: ordinary, well drained but not dry

Height: 15 cm (6 in)

Spread: 23 cm (9 in)

Type of plant: hardy annual

Flowers: rounded, blue or blue and white blooms

Flowering time: summer

Sowing time: spring (outdoors where plants are to flower); thin seedlings to 10 cm (4 in) when large enough to handle; can also sow in autumn to flower earlier the following summer

Species cultivated: *N. insignis* (syn. *menziesii*) is the most popular kind and it has pale blue flowers with white centres; *N. maculata* (photograph) is less widely grown but its flowers of white, spotted with purple, are very attractive

Cultivation and uses: although it will grow in sunny places this plant does like a moist soil; it will not tolerate being sun-baked. Grow it in semi-shady pockets on the rock garden, as an edging to beds and borders and alongside paths

Tobacco Plant
Nicotiana

Site: sunny or partially shady

Soil: ordinary, fertile

Height: 30 to 90 cm (1 to 3 ft)

Spread: 30 to 60 cm (1 to 2 ft)

Type of plant: half-hardy annual

Flowers: large flat-ended trumpets of red, yellow, pink, pale green and white. Fragrant

Flowering time: summer to early autumn

Sowing time: spring (under glass, 15°C, 59°F), outdoors in frost-free climates only

Planting time: early summer, when danger of frost is past

Planting distance: 23 to 30 cm (9 in to 1 ft)

Species cultivated: *N. alata* (syn *N. affinis*) (photograph) is the parent of most of today's annual sweet-scented tobacco plants; recommended varieties: 'Sensation Mixed' 75 cm (2½ ft), 'Dwarf Idol' 30 cm (1 ft), crimson, 'Evening Fragrance' 90 cm (3 ft), mixed, particularly fragrant, 'Lime Green' 60 cm (2 ft), pale green

Cultivation and uses: in warmer climates the plants may survive for a few years but they are normally treated as annuals and raised afresh from seed each spring. Good plants to give height to the annual border. Flowers last well in water and the green variety is particularly popular with flower arrangers

Love-in-a-mist
Nigella

Site: sunny

Soil: ordinary

Height: 30 to 45 cm (12 to 18 in)

Spread: 23 cm (9 in)

Type of plant: hardy annual

Flowers: blooms like cornflowers surrounded by feathery leaves. Pink, blue and white

Flowering time: summer

Sowing time: spring (outdoors where plants are to flower). Thin seedlings to 15 cm (6 in) when large enough to handle. Can also be sown in autumn to make larger plants which flower a little sooner

Species cultivated: *N. damascena* also known as devil-in-a-bush is the parent of the most popular varieties: 'Miss Jekyll' blue, and 'Persian Jewels' (photograph) mixed

Cultivation and uses: no particular requirements; excellent for filling gaps in beds and borders and for growing in dry patches of soil. The seedheads are decorative when dried

Poppy
Papaver

Site: sunny

Soil: ordinary, well drained

Height: 45 to 75 cm (18 to 30 in)

Spread: 15 to 23 cm (6 to 9 in)

Type of plant: hardy annual

Flowers: large double or single blooms in shades of red, orange, yellow pink and white

Flowering time: summer

Sowing time: late spring (outdoors where the plants are to flower); thin seedlings to 15 cm (6 in) when large enough to handle; may also be sown in autumn to flower slightly earlier the following summer

Species cultivated: the varieties most easily available are derived from *P. rhoeas* and *P. somniferum*; recommended varieties: 'Shirley Mixed' 75 cm (30 in), double (photograph) or single mixtures, 'Ladybird' 45 cm (18 in), single scarlet and black, 'Pink Chiffon' 75 cm (30 in), double pink, 'San Remo' 60 cm (24 in), single mixed

Cultivation and uses: no special requirements. Excellent cottage garden plants which also look well in annual beds and borders

Geranium
Pelargonium

Site: sunny

Soil: ordinary, well drained

Height: 30 to 60 cm (1 to 2 ft)

Spread: 30 cm (1 ft)

Type of plant: half-hardy perennial

Flowers: white, pink, orange and scarlet

Flowering time: almost all the year round

Sowing time: winter (under glass, 20°C, 68°F) pot on as they grow until planting out time

Planting time: early summer, when danger of frost is past

Planting distance: 30 cm (1 ft)

Species cultivated: *P. zonale* is the species from which the seed-raised varieties have been derived; recommended varieties: Del Greco Hybrids, in single and mixed colours, Sprinter Mixture, Ringo, vivid scarlet, Carefree Mixed

Cultivation and uses: normally raised from cuttings but these varieties may be propagated from seeds. They can be grown all the year round as pot plants but are also bedded out in the summer; they should be potted up and brought indoors before the first frosts. In the first summer after sowing they will make many leaves and few flowers but will continue flowering through the winter if potted up

Beard Tongue

Penstemon

Site: sunny, sheltered

Soil: fertile, well drained

Height: 60 to 75 cm (24 to 30 in)

Spread: 23 to 30 cm (9 to 12 in)

Type of plant: half-hardy perennial

Flowers: bell-shaped blooms of pink, lilac, purple and red variously marked with white

Flowering time: summer to autumn

Sowing time: late winter (under glass, 15°C, 59°F). Can also be sown in summer outdoors to produce flowers the following year

Planting time: early summer, when danger of frost is past

Planting distance: 30 cm (12 in)

Species cultivated: most of the garden hybrids go under the general name of *P. gloxinioides*; recommended varieties: various good strains are sold as Large-flowered Mixed (photograph)

Cultivation and uses: the plants are hardy only in the mildest of winters in cool climates so to be sure of their survival take cuttings in late summer and cover plants left outdoors with straw or bracken; in frost-free climates they will survive without this protection; good plants to give height to beds and borders

Petunia

Petunia

Site: sunny

Soil: ordinary, well drained

Height: 15 to 30 cm (6 to 12 in)

Spread: 15 to 23 cm (6 to 9 in)

Type of plant: half-hardy annual

Flowers: large single trumpets or frilly double flowers in single colours or combinations of red, white, pink, purple, cerise, magenta and yellow

Flowering time: summer to autumn

Sowing time: late winter to early spring (under glass, 15°C, 59°F), outdoors in frost-free climates only

Planting time: early summer (when danger of frost is past)

Planting distance: 15 to 23 cm (6 to 9 in)

Species cultivated: the annual varieties of today are hybrids between *P. integrifolia* and *P. nictaginiflora* and are known as either *grandiflora* (large-flowered) or *multiflora* (many-flowered) types; recommended varieties: 'Pacesetter' 30 cm (12 in), rich rose (photograph), 'Brass Band' 30 cm (12 in), rich rose yellow, 'Colour Parade' 30 cm (12 in), large-flowered mixed, 'Ricochet' 23 cm (9 in) rose pink with white stripes

Cultivation and uses: no special requirements; excellent long-flowering plants for the front of beds and borders and for planting in pots, hanging baskets and window-boxes

Phlox

Phlox

Site: sunny

Soil: fertile, well drained

Height: 15 to 30 cm (6 to 12 in)

Spread: 15 to 23 cm (6 to 9 in)

Type of plant: half-hardy annual

Flowers: blue, purple, pink, red and white, many of the darker colours having a white eye

Flowering time: summer

Sowing time: late winter or early spring (under glass, 13°C, 55°F); may also be sown under glass in late autumn and planted out the following spring; spring outdoors in frost-free climates only

Planting time: late spring to early summer when danger of frost is past

Planting distance: 15 cm (6 in)

Species cultivated: the annual varieties are derived from *P. drummondii*; recommended varieties: 'Large-flowered Mixed' (photograph) 30 cm (12 in), 'Dwarf Beauty' 15 cm (6 in), mixed

Cultivation and uses: pinch out the tops of the plants when they are planted out to encourage bushiness; good in annual beds and borders, alongside paths and in pots and window-boxes. Flowers last well in water

Coneflower

Rudbeckia

Site: sunny

Soil: ordinary, well drained

Height: 45 to 90 cm (18 to 36 in)

Spread: 30 to 60 cm (12 to 24 in)

Type of plant: half-hardy annual

Flowers: large daisies with a prominent central boss; yellow, orange, mahogany

Flowering time: summer to autumn

Sowing time: late winter to early spring (under glass, 15°C, 59°F); can also be sown in early summer under glass and planted out in autumn or spring to flower earlier the following summer; sow in spring outdoors in frost-free climates only

Planting time: early summer

Planting distance: 23 to 30 cm (9 to 12 in)

Species cultivated: the annual varieties are derived from several species including *R. hirta*; recommended varieties: 'Golden Flame' (photograph) 45 cm (18 in), bright yellow, 'Marmalade' 45 cm (18 in), rich yellow, 'Rustic Dwarfs' 60 cm (2 ft), yellow, orange and mahogany

Cultivation and uses: stake the taller varieties with twiggy branches. Not strictly an annual and may survive mild winters or frost-free climates to flower again the following year. Flowers last well in water

Painted Tongue
Salpiglossis

Site: sunny

Soil: ordinary, fertile

Height: 60 cm (2 ft)

Spread: 30 cm (1 ft)

Type of plant: half-hardy annual

Flowers: beautifully veined trumpet-shaped blooms in shades of red, yellow, orange, blue and violet

Flowering time: summer

Sowing time: late winter to early spring (under glass, 15°C, 59°F), outdoors in frost-free climates only

Planting time: early summer, when danger of frost is past

Planting distance: 23 cm (9 in)

Species cultivated: *S. sinuata* is the species from which today's mixed varieties are derived; the best of these are: 'Bolero' (photograph) and 'Triumph Mixed'; 'Shalimar' is a large-flowered variety which has a second flush of bloom in late summer

Cultivation and uses: may also be grown in pots as a cool greenhouse plant and in containers outdoors through the summer; plants should be staked with twiggy branches in both pots and flower beds

Sage, Clary
Salvia

Site: sunny

Soil: ordinary, well drained

Height: 23 to 45 cm (9 to 18 in)

Spread: 23 cm (9 in)

Type of plant: hardy annual and half-hardy annual

Flowers: scarlet sage has bright red spikes of bloom, though purple and cerise versions are also available. The annual clary has coloured bracts which range through purple and pink to white

Flowering time: summer to autumn

Sowing time: annual clary: spring (outdoors); thin seedlings when large enough to handle to leave one every 15 cm (6 in); scarlet sage: late winter to early spring (under glass, 18°C, 65°F), outdoors in frost-free climates only

Planting time: early summer, when danger of frost is past (for plants raised under glass)

Planting distance: 23 cm (9 in)

Species cultivated: *S. splendens* is the scarlet sage and there are a number of varieties. *S. horminum* (photograph) is the annual clary and is sold in mixed or single-coloured varieties

Cultivation and uses: no special requirements. Both are excellent plants for beds and borders

Pincushion Flower, Scabious

Scabiosa

Site: sunny

Soil: ordinary, fertile, appreciate lime

Height: 45 to 75 cm (18 to 30 in)

Spread: 30 cm (12 in)

Type of plant: hardy annual

Flowers: rounded and rather fluffy blooms of blue, mauve, crimson, pink and white

Flowering time: summer to autumn

Sowing time: late spring (outdoors where the plants are to flower); thin the seedlings when large enough to handle to leave one every 23 cm (9 in); may also be sown outdoors in autumn to flower earlier the following summer

Species cultivated: *S. atropurpurea* (photograph) is the parent of the annual kinds which are sold in mixed varieties of varying heights

Cultivation and uses: stake plants with twiggy branches; excellent plants for sowing in large or small drifts in beds and borders

Poor Man's Orchid

Schizanthus

Site: sunny

Soil: ordinary, well drained

Height: 15 to 120 cm (6 to 48 in)

Spread: 15 to 30 cm (6 to 12 in)

Type of plant: half-hardy annual

Flowers: delicately marked blooms of pink, mauve, cream, violet and white

Flowering time: spring and summer

Sowing time: spring (to flower in summer), autumn (to flower in spring), under glass, 15°C, 59°F; spring outdoors in frost-free climates only

Planting time: early summer when danger of frost is past

Planting distance: 15 cm (6 in)

Species cultivated: *S. wisetonensis* (photograph) is the parent of today's varieties, though it is a hybrid itself. Recommended varieties: 'Hit Parade' 30 cm (1 ft), 'Pansy Flowered' 30 to 75 cm (12 to 30 in), larger blooms but not delicately marked, 'Star Parade' 15 cm (6 in), a new dwarf variety. All are mixed

Cultivation and uses: although it can be bedded out in summer, the Poor Man's Orchid is usually grown as a cool greenhouse pot plant. Three or four plants will fit in a 13-cm (5-in) pot. Whether grown in pots or the open ground the plants should be staked with twiggy branches

African or French Marigold
Tagetes

Site: sunny

Soil: ordinary, fertile

Height: 15 to 90 cm (6 to 36 in)

Spread: 15 to 23 cm (6 to 9 in)

Type of plant: half-hardy annual

Flowers: large or small, double or single in shades of yellow, orange and mahogany

Flowering time: summer to autumn

Sowing time: early spring (under glass, 15°C, 59°F), outdoors in frost-free climates only

Planting time: early summer, when danger of frost is past

Planting distance: 15 to 23 cm (6 to 9 in)

Species cultivated: *T. erecta* is the African marigold, varieties include 'First Lady' 45 cm (18 in), bright yellow, 'Orange Climax' 100 cm (3 ft), bright orange. French marigolds are derived from *T. patula*, varieties include 'Cinnabar' 30 cm (1 ft), mahogany, single, 'Goldfinch' 20 cm (8 in), bright yellow; *T. tenuifolia pumila* is the smallest of the tagetes grown for bedding, varieties include 'Tangerine Gem' 23 cm (9 in), orange, 'Paprika' 15 cm (6 in), mahogany with yellow-edged petals

Cultivation and uses: the African types are good plants for beds and borders and the other two make good edging plants; all the smaller varieties are suitable for planting in window-boxes

Mexican Sunflower
Tithonia

Site: sunny

Soil: ordinary

Height: 100 to 120 cm (3 to 4 ft)

Spread: 45 cm (18 in)

Type of plant: half-hardy annual

Flowers: large single 'daisies', usually orange

Flowering time: summer

Sowing time: spring (under glass, 13°C, 55°F), outdoors in frost-free climates only

Planting time: early summer, as soon as danger of frost is past

Planting distance: 35 cm (15 in)

Species cultivated: *T. rotundifolia* (syn. *T. speciosa*) is available in a limited range of varieties, the most popular of which is 'Torch' with orange-red blooms

Cultivation and uses: stake the plants to prevent them from toppling over – twiggy branches will be unobtrusive yet effective; the flowers last well in water

Nasturtium

Tropaeolum

Site: sunny

Soil: ordinary

Height: 23 to 120 cm (9 in to 4 ft)

Spread: 45 to 200 cm (18 in to 6 ft)

Type of plant: hardy annual

Flowers: large single trumpets or double blooms in shades of red, orange and yellow

Flowering time: summer to autumn

Sowing time: spring, outdoors; space-sow the seeds 15 cm (6 in) apart or at the foot of supports for climbing kinds.

Sowing time: spring, outdoors; space-sow the seeds varieties include 'Golden Gleam' 30 cm (1 ft), bright yellow, 'Red Roulette' 23 cm (9 in), scarlet, 'Alaska' 23 cm (9 in) mixed flowers and variegated foliage, 'Whirlybird Mixed' 23 cm (9 in), spur-less flowers held well clear of the foliage; there are many good climbing and trailing types which are usually sold in mixed colours

Cultivation and uses: avoid planting nasturtiums in very rich soil or they will produce more leaf than flower. The trailing and bushy nasturtiums are excellent edging plants and look well planted on the tops of hollow walls. The flowers last well in water

Ursinia

Ursinia

Site: sunny and sheltered

Soil: light, well drained

Height: 30 to 45 cm (12 to 18 in)

Spread: 23 to 30 cm (9 to 12 in)

Type of plant: half-hardy annual

Flowers: yellow or orange 'daisies' carried on stiff stalks

Flowering time: summer

Sowing time: spring (under glass, 18°C, 65°F), outdoors in frost-free climates only

Planting time: early summer, when danger of frost is past

Planting distance: 15 cm (6 in)

Species cultivated: *U. anethoides* (photograph) is the kind most easily obtainable; it has orange flowers with a purple central zone; mixed hybrids are also sold and these have flowers in various shades of yellow and orange and occasionally a few reds

Cultivation and uses: good plants for warm, sunny borders and the edges of paths

Venidium
Venidium

Site: sunny and sheltered

Soil: ordinary, well drained

Height: 60 to 90 cm (2 to 3 ft)

Spread: 30 cm (1 ft)

Type of plant: half-hardy annual

Flowers: large orange 'daisies' with a dark central boss

Flowering time: summer

Sowing time: spring (under glass, 15°C, 59°F), outdoors in frost-free climates only

Planting time: early summer, when danger of frost is past

Planting distance: 23 cm (9 in)

Species cultivated: *V. fastuosum* (photograph) is the kind most widely available. The orange-yellow flowers are 10 cm (4 in) or so in diameter

Cultivation and uses: no special requirements. Good plants for sunny beds and borders

Vervain
Verbena

Site: sunny

Soil: ordinary, fertile

Height: 15 to 30 cm (6 to 12 in)

Spread: 23 to 30 cm (9 to 12 in)

Type of plant: half-hardy annual

Flowers: showy heads of red, pink, mauve, violet, purple and white

Flowering time: summer to autumn

Sowing time: early spring (under glass, 15°C, 59°F), outdoors in frost-free climates only

Planting time: early summer, when danger of frost is past

Planting distance: 15 to 23 cm (6 to 9 in)

Species cultivated: *V. hybrida* (photograph) is the best tender kind and it has many varieties including: 'Rainbow Mixed' 23 cm (9 in), early to come into flower, 'Dwarf Compact Mixed' 15 cm (6 in), 'Amethyst' 23 cm (9 in), violet with white eye, 'Delight' 15 cm (6 in), pink

Cultivation and uses: these plants are really perennials but are almost always raised afresh each year from seed or cuttings. Plant them in annual beds and borders and alongside paths where their sprawling habit can be used to advantage. They are good subjects for planting in pots either in the cool greenhouse or outdoors

Pansy
Viola

Site: sunny or partially shady

Soil: ordinary, fertile

Height: 15 to 23 cm (6 to 9 in)

Spread: 15 to 30 cm (6 to 12 in)

Type of plant: hardy biennial

Flowers: white, blue, red, yellow, violet and purple, many with deep purple markings

Flowering time: spring to late autumn

Sowing time: summer (in cold frame or unheated greenhouse) to raise plants for spring flowering; spring (under glass, 13°C, 55°F,) to raise plants for summer flowers

Planting time: autumn (for spring flowering), late spring (for summer flowering)

Planting distance: 15 cm (6 in)

Species cultivated: most of today's pansies are hybrids of *V. × wittrockiana* and come in an assortment of single and mixed colours. 'Azure Blue' is the illustrated variety

Cultivation and uses: although treated as biennials, pansies are really short-lived perennials. They seed themselves freely. Use them as an edging to beds and paths and plant them with spring-flowering bulbs such as tulips (photograph)

Rose of Heaven
Viscaria

Site: sunny

Soil: ordinary

Height: 30 cm (1 ft)

Spread: 23 to 30 cm (9 to 12 in)

Type of plant: hardy annual

Flowers: wide open blooms of blue, pink or white

Flowering time: summer

Sowing time: spring (outdoors where plants are to flower). Thin seedlings to 15 cm (6 in) when large enough to handle. May also be sown in autumn (outdoors) to flower earlier the following summer

Species cultivated: the naming of this plant is very confused. It is correctly known as *Lychnis coeli-rosa* but is often found under various other names including *Silene coeli-rosa* and *Agrostemma coeli-rosa*. However, it is to be found in the catalogues of seedsmen listed as *Viscaria oculata* and may be offered in the following varieties: Oculata Mixed, (photograph); Brilliant Mixture; 'Love' rose pink; 'Blue Angel' mid blue

Cultivation and uses: good plants for sunny spots in beds and borders

Xeranthemum

Xeranthemum

Site: sunny

Soil: ordinary, well drained

Height: 60 cm (2 ft)

Spread: 23 to 30 cm (9 to 12 in)

Type of plant: hardy annual

Flowers: double or single everlasting 'daisy' flowers in shades of purple, pink and white

Flowering time: summer

Sowing time: spring (outdoors where the plants are to flower). Thin seedlings to 15 cm (6 in) when large enough to handle

Species cultivated: *X. annuum* (photograph) is the species from which all available varieties have been derived. Recommended varieties: many mixed selections are offered and these include both double- and single-flowered plants. 'Amethyst' is a double-flowered variety with deep rose-coloured blooms

Cultivation and uses: stake the plants with twiggy branches if the site is at all exposed. Pick the flowers when they are at their best and dry them for winter decoration. Dried flowers retain their colour well

Youth and Old Age

Zinnia

Site: sunny and sheltered

Soil: fertile, well drained

Height: 15 to 75 cm (6 to 30 in)

Spread: 15 to 30 cm (6 to 12 in)

Type of plant: half-hardy annual

Flowers: large double or semi-double 'daisy' flowers in shades of red, pink, mauve, orange, yellow, carmine, green and white. Some strains are bi-coloured

Flowering time: summer

Sowing time: spring (under glass, 18°C, 65°F), outdoors in frost-free climates only

Planting time: early summer, when danger of frost is past

Planting distance: 23 to 30 cm (9 to 12 in)

Species cultivated: *Z. elegans* is the parent of today's garden varieties of which the following are recommended: 'Ruffles Mixture' 60 cm (2 ft), particularly full flowers, 'Yellow Ruffles' (photograph) 60 cm (2 ft), bright yellow, 'Envy', 45 cm (18 in), acid green. There are many other mixed and single-coloured varieties

Cultivation and uses: the plants resent any check to growth so sow them in late spring if conditions look like being unfavourable for early planting, alternatively sow them outdoors in early summer and thin

Rock Garden Plants

Plants for the rock garden are of many different kinds, low-growing perennials or tiny shrubs, bulbs or dwarf conifers. And, of course, there are the true alpines – plants which occur naturally in mountainous regions at high altitudes. Excessive rain and wetness at the roots are the major killers of the true alpine plant – and it may be much more satisfactory to grow these in pots or pans which can be housed in a frame or greenhouse.

Warmer, frost-free climates are not ideal for rock plants and, indeed, they are only suitable for regions where the summers are not too hot. They must then be given some protection from sun and wind.

One of the nice things about rock plants is the number of ways there are in which they can be grown and displayed. You can have a traditional rock garden such as I have myself, set on falling ground and incorporating a water feature, or you can grow them in raised beds – very popular and especially useful in small gardens nowadays. Then they can be grown in trough or sink gardens or in dry stone walls and steps. Whichever you choose I am sure that you are going to get a lot of pleasure from the plants you grow, for rock plants include many of great beauty.

Making the rock garden

Let's start with the rock garden proper. The great art of building one of these is to try and give it the appearance of a natural outcrop, and this is largely achieved by making the strata lines on the rocks you use all run in the same direction – just as they would in nature. Just as in nature, too, most of each piece of rock should be hidden from view. I would advise using stone from your own locality whenever possible, for it will work out a lot cheaper that way and is likely to look much more natural.

You will, of course, arrange things so that you end up with a series of planting pockets and these can, if so desired, be filled with soil especially suited for particular plants – alkaline mixtures for the lime-loving plants, acid mixtures for the lime haters. Generally speaking, though, it will be a case of making use of the ordinary garden soil and improving this as necessary. Peat is a great help in this respect, improving the soil texture and moisture-holding capacity without in any way interfering with free drainage. On heavier soils, too, I would suggest working-in coarse sand to make it more workable and amenable to the plants' roots.

Many rock garden plants can be bought in pots so planting can be done at any time of the year, when the conditions are suitable. This usually means avoiding summer if it is very dry and winter when frost is on the ground.

Raised beds

The raised, or rock, bed is, perhaps, a better and more practical proposition in the small garden, and in the garden which is already so committed for space in other directions that there really isn't room to fit a rock garden in. That is nothing to be despondent about for a bed of this kind can be extraordinarily attractive and satisfying when well planted. Its low stone walls are not difficult to build, and the only real concern is to ensure that provision is made for really free drainage. Alpine plants from high altitudes will, naturally, stand any amount of cold; what they will not put up with is cold combined with wetness at the roots. Similarly, some alpines are very sensitive to winter wet, especially those plants with woolly leaves like the well-known edelweiss, *Leontopodium alpinum*. Such plants need to be given the protection of a pane of glass in winter.

Obviously, with such a rock bed the soil mixture used will be suited to the special needs of the plants in which you are interested. Rocks can be incorporated (of a size suited to the scale of the planting overall), but it may well be better to keep everything 'on the flat' and reproduce scree conditions, even to the extent of covering the soil with a thin layer of stone chippings. These always look attractive and help to keep down weeds, but you must not, of course, use limestone chippings if you are growing lime-hating plants.

A sink garden

The growing of rock plants (or at least the smaller and not too vigorous kinds) in troughs or sinks has long been popular. Again, you must be very careful to provide enough drainage, which means at least one sizeable hole in the base of the container towards which excess water can freely drain. This is covered with crocks or a piece of perforated gauze before the compost is added. Another thing you must not overlook is the need for the container to have a fair amount of depth. I would consider 10 cm (4 in) of soil the absolute minimum for satisfactory growth.

Dry walls

Dry walls are a delightful garden feature planted with a variety of suitable plants. Aubrietas and alyssums immediately spring to mind and, of course, there are many more including helianthemums, sempervivums and saxifrages. Such a wall does not only provide innumerable planting stations on its face but it also usually makes provision for rock plants to be grown on its top.

Propagation

Division is the most usual way of increasing rock plants, though some can be increased by cuttings rooted in pans filled with sandy compost and placed in a cold frame or in shade outdoors, or by rooted offsets detached from their parent plants. Seed is another method of increase for certain species and selected strains.

A traditional rock garden

A raised bed is an attractive alternative
to a rock garden

A dry wall can be built against a soil
bank or may be free standing with
a central soil cavity

Sink gardens must be provided with
good drainage

Acaena

Acaena

Site: sunny or partially shady

Soil: ordinary, well drained

Height: 8 to 10 cm (3 to 4 in)

Spread: 45 cm (18 in)

Flowers: uninteresting, but large, reddish 'burrs' that follow are very decorative

Flowering time: summer

Planting time: spring to autumn

Propagation: sow seeds under glass in spring; divide mature plants in spring or autumn

Recommended species: *A. buchananii* (photograph) grey-green leaves and red burrs; *A. microphylla*, blue-grey to bronze leaves and crimson burrs; *A. novae-zelandiae*, blue-grey to bronze leaves and purple burrs

Cultivation and uses: easy plants to grow provided that the soil is well drained and they are not subjected to a great deal of winter moisture; good ground-cover plants which look well in light shade under trees or in cracks among paving stones

Pheasant's Eye

Adonis

Site: sunny

Soil: rich, well drained, limy

Height: 30 to 45 cm (12 to 18 in)

Spread: 30 cm (1 ft)

Flowers: large double or single yellow 'daisy' flowers

Flowering time: spring

Planting time: spring or autumn

Propagation: sow seeds under glass as soon as they are available; divide mature plants in spring or autumn

Recommended species: *A. amurensis*, 30 cm (1 ft), yellow (the variety *flore pleno* has double flowers); *A. vernalis* (photograph), 45 cm (18 in), yellow

Cultivation and uses: these perennial adonises are quite small and dainty when in flower during spring but their foliage grows quickly afterwards to take the plants to their ultimate size; plant them in spacious pockets of good soil in the rock garden

Madwort, Gold Dust
Alyssum

Site: sunny

Soil: ordinary, well drained

Height: 10 to 30 cm (4 in to 1 ft)

Spread: up to 1 m (3 ft)

Flowers: large heads of yellow blooms

Flowering time: spring and summer

Planting time: spring or autumn

Propagation: sow seeds under glass in spring; take cuttings of firm young growths in summer

Recommended species: *A. montanum*, 8 to 10 cm (3 to 4 in), bright yellow, scented; *A. saxatile* (gold dust) 30 cm (1 ft), bright yellow, varieties 'Dudley Neville' (photograph) creamy yellow, 'Citrinum' lemon yellow, *flore pleno* double yellow

Cultivation and uses: no special requirements; superb plants for positioning on top of rocks and walls so that their stems and flower trusses are allowed to cascade over the edge; good also as an edging to sunny beds and borders

Rock Cress
Arabis

Site: sunny

Soil: ordinary

Height: 10 to 15 cm (4 to 6 in) but trailing in habit

Spread: up to 1 m (3 ft)

Flowers: single or double blooms of white or pink

Flowering time: spring and early summer

Planting time: spring or autumn

Propagation: sow seeds outdoors in summer; take cuttings of healthy young growths in summer; divide mature plants in autumn

Recommended species: *A. albida* (photograph) white, and varieties *flore pleno* double, 'Rosabella' pink, *variegata* yellow-variegated leaves; *A. ferdinandi-coburgii variegata*, white flowers and variegated leaves

Cultivation and uses: easy plant to grow in sunny spots on rock gardens, walls and alongside paths; it also thrives in sunny beds and borders where it can be used as a carpeter and interplanted with spring-flowering bulbs such as tulips or daffodils

Purple Rock Cress

Aubrieta

Site: sunny

Soil: ordinary

Height: 8 to 10 cm (3 to 4 in) trailing habit

Spread: up to 1 m (3 ft)

Flowers: single, four-petalled flowers of red, crimson, mauve, pink, lilac, violet and purple

Flowering time: spring and early summer

Planting time: spring or autumn

Propagation: sow seeds outdoors in spring; take cuttings of healthy young shoot tips in summer; divide mature plants in spring

Recommended species: *A. deltoidea* is grown in a wide range of varieties and among the best of these are: 'Belisha Beacon' rose red, 'Dr Mules' violet purple, 'Dream' pale bluish purple, 'Joan Allen' crimson and double, *variegata*, pale blue flowers and variegated leaves

Cultivation and uses: keep the plants in good condition and prevent straggly bare stems by lightly clipping them over when the flowers have faded; sunny borders and beds can be edged with aubrieta and it also looks superb in large drifts on the rock garden or when it is planted on top of walls so that it can cascade over the edge; renew the plants every few years when they wear themselves out

Bellflower

Campanula carpatica

Site: sunny

Soil: ordinary, well drained

Height: 15 to 30 cm (6 to 12 in)

Spread: 30 cm (12 in)

Flowers: bells of white, blue or purple

Flowering time: summer

Planting time: spring or autumn

Propagation: sow seeds outdoors in spring; divide mature plants in autumn

Recommended species: *C. carpatica* (photograph) has a number of excellent varieties; 'Alba' 30 cm (12 in), white; 'Blue Moonlight' 25 cm (10 in), pale blue; 'Isobel' 25 cm (10 in), deep blue

Cultivation and uses: water well in very dry weather; excellent for planting in sunny pockets in the rock garden and at the front of beds and borders as an edging

Bellflower

Campanula portenschlagiana

Site: sunny

Site: ordinary, well drained

Height: up to 15 cm (6 in)

Spread: up to 50 cm (20 in)

Flowers: purple on trailing stems

Flowering time: summer and autumn

Planting time: spring or autumn

Propagation: sow seeds outdoors in spring; divide mature plants in autumn

Recommended species: the variety *C. portenschlagiana* 'Major' has larger flowers than the species. C. 'Birch Hybrid' (photograph) is a hybrid from *C. portenschlagiana* and *C. poscharskyana*. The latter grows to 30 cm (12 in) and has lavender blue flowers

Cultivation and uses: a sprawling plant suitable for the rock garden, edging borders and planting in path or wall crevices; water well in dry weather

Snow-in-summer

Cerastium

Site: sunny

Soil: ordinary, well drained

Height: 8 to 15 cm (3 to 6 in)

Spread: up to 1.25 or 1.5 m (4 or 5 ft)

Flowers: white, star shaped

Flowering time: late spring to early summer

Planting time: spring or autumn

Propagation: divide mature plants in spring

Recommended species: *C. alpinum*, 8 cm (3 in), not invasive; *C. biebersteinii* (photograph), 15 cm (6 in); *C. tomentosum*, 15 cm (6 in), very invasive but a good garden plant, this variety is the one most commonly grown

Cultivation and uses: cut the plants back severely if they become too invasive, but better still give them plenty of room in the first place. The two vigorous species which need this treatment also look well planted in walls so that they can trail their stems over the edge; otherwise grow all three species in pockets in the rock garden

Maiden Pink
Dianthus deltoides

Site: sunny

Soil: ordinary, well drained; thrives in chalky soil

Height: 10 to 20 cm (4 to 8 in)

Spread: 10 cm (4 in)

Flowers: red to pink to white

Flowering time: summer

Planting time: spring or autumn

Propagation: sow seeds outdoors in spring; take cuttings of firm young growths in summer; divide mature plants in spring

Recommended species: *D. deltoides* (photograph) has a number of varieties; 'Albus' white; 'Brilliant' crimson; 'Erectus' deep red

Cultivation and uses: lift and divide clumps when they become old and worn out; excellent for sunny pockets in the rock garden, for planting on walls and for edging sunny, well-drained beds and borders; flowers last well in water

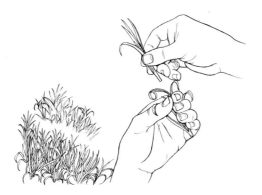

Taking a cutting

Pink
Dianthus plumarius

Site: sunny

Soil: ordinary, well drained; thrive in chalky soil

Height: 15 to 30 cm (6 to 12 in)

Spread: 20 cm (8 in)

Flowers: pink, white, red or bi-colour according to variety

Flowering time: summer

Planting time: spring or autumn

Propagation: for varieties take cuttings of firm young growths in summer; divide mature plants in spring;

Recommended species: *D. plumarius* itself is rarely grown today, but many of its varieties are: these fall into four groups:
(1) selfs (one colour)
(2) bi-colours (eye of flower a different colour)
(3) laced
(4) fancies (irregular colour markings)

Cultivation and uses: lift and divide clumps when they become old and worn out; excellent for sunny borders

Mountain Avens

Dryas

Site: sunny

Soil: well drained with grit added

Height: 10 cm (4 in)

Spread: up to 60 cm (2 ft)

Flowers: white or yellow blooms which have a yellow central boss of stigma and stamens

Flowering time: late spring and early summer

Planting time: spring or autumn

Propagation: sow seeds in a cool greenhouse in spring; take cuttings of firm young growths in autumn; divide mature plants in spring

Recommended species: *D. drummondii* yellow; *D. octopetala* (photograph) creamy white; *D. suendermannii* cream, fading to white; all three are ground hugging

Cultivation and uses: excellent for warm spots in the rock garden where they can be positioned to tumble over large boulders; they are long-lived and will form a thick carpet

Gentian

Gentiana

Site: sunny or partially shady

Soil: well drained but peaty and lime-free

Height: 8 to 30 cm (3 to 12 in)

Spread: 15 to 45 cm (6 to 18 in)

Flowers: blue or white trumpet-shaped

Flowering time: spring to summer and autumn

Planting time: spring

Propagation: sow seeds under glass in spring (may take over a year to germinate); divide mature plants in spring

Recommended species: *G. acaulis*, 10 cm (4 in), deep blue, spring; *G. farreri*, 8 cm (3 in), blue and white, late summer to autumn; *G. septemfida*, 23 to 30 cm (9 to 12 in), blue, summer; *G. sino-ornata*, 8 cm (3 in), deep blue, autumn, and variety 'Alba', white; *G. verna* (photograph), 5 cm (2 in), rich blue, spring

Cultivation and uses: though most gentians dislike lime, *G. acaulis* and one or two others will tolerate an alkaline soil. All species prefer a rich well-drained soil and will appreciate an annual mulch of decayed manure, garden compost or peat in spring. Grow the species mentioned here in pockets in the rock garden and try to keep them free of excessive moisture in the winter months

Sun Rose

Helianthemum

Site: sunny

Soil: ordinary, well drained

Height: 23 to 30 cm (9 to 12 in)

Spread: 1 m (3 ft) and more

Flowers: rounded, wide open blooms of white, yellow, orange, pink or red. Some double varieties

Flowering time: summer

Planting time: spring or autumn

Propagation: sow seeds under glass in spring; take cuttings of firm young growths in summer

Recommended species: most of the good garden varieties of today are derived from *H. nummularium*, 23 to 30 cm (9 to 12 in), yellow; among the best of these varieties are: 'The Bride' white, 'Wisley Pink' soft pink, 'Golden Queen' rich yellow, 'Lawrenson's Pink' (photograph), 'Firedragon' orange-red, 'Jubilee' double yellow, 'Ben Ledi' crimson, 'Ben Afflick' cream and orange

Cultivation and uses: prune the bushes lightly after flowering to keep them in shape. Excellent plants for sunny parts of the rock garden and for growing on banks and in walls so that their stems can tumble downwards displaying the flowers to full effect

Perennial Candytuft

Iberis

Site: sunny

Soil: ordinary, well drained

Height: 15 to 30 cm (6 to 12 in)

Spread: 1 m (3 ft) or more

Flowers: close-packed heads of small white blooms

Flowering time: late spring and early summer

Planting time: spring or autumn

Propagation: sow seeds in a cool greenhouse in spring; take cuttings of firm young growths in summer; divide mature plants in spring

Recommended species: *I. saxatilis*, 15 cm (6 in); *I. sempervirens* (photograph), 23 to 30 cm (9 to 12 in), and varieties 'Little Gem' 15 cm (6 in), slow growing, and 'Snowflake' 23 to 30 cm (9 to 12 in), the most popular variety

Cultivation and uses: dig up and divide the plants when they become too rampant and exhausted (though this will not be for some years); excellent in large pockets on the rock garden, on banks and at the front of sunny and well-drained beds and borders

Edelweiss

Leontopodium

Site: sunny

Soil: gritty and well drained

Height: 10 to 15 cm (4 to 6 in)

Spread: 15 to 23 cm (6 to 9 in)

Flowers: small yellow blooms surrounded by greyish-white woolly bracts

Flowering time: summer

Planting time: spring

Propagation: sow seeds in spring in a cool greenhouse; divide mature plants in spring

Recommended species: *L. alpinum* (photograph) is the only variety widely cultivated

Cultivation and uses: a modestly spectacular plant for a sunny and well-drained spot in the rock garden. It will not stand excessive winter moisture and should be protected with a pane of glass. Flowers can be dried for winter decoration

Flax

Linum

Site: sunny, sheltered

Soil: ordinary, well drained

Height: 15 to 60 cm (6 in to 2 ft)

Spread: 30 to 60 cm (1 to 2 ft)

Flowers: large wide-open blooms of blue, yellow or white

Flowering time: summer

Planting time: spring or autumn

Propagation: sow seeds outdoors in early summer; divide mature plants in spring

Recommended species: *L. alpinum*, 15 cm (6 in), blue; *L. flavum* (photograph), 30 to 45 cm (12 to 18 in), bright yellow; *L. narbonnense*, 60 cm (2 ft), blue; *L. perenne*, 45 cm (18 in), blue; *L. monogynum*, 45 cm (18 in), white

Cultivation and uses: cut down dead stems in winter. Superb plants for massing together in large drifts on the rock garden or in sunny borders; look well planted in walls

Gromwell
Lithospermum

Site: sunny, sheltered

Soil: ordinary, well drained, lime-free

Height: 10 to 15 cm (4 to 6 in)

Spread: 30 to 60 cm (1 to 2 ft)

Flowers: starry blooms of blue or white

Flowering time: summer

Planting time: spring or autumn

Propagation: sow seeds in a cool greenhouse in spring; take cuttings of firm young growths in summer; layer healthy trailing shoots in spring or autumn

Recommended species: *L. diffusum* (photograph) is the species most commonly grown; good varieties of this species are: 'Grace Ward' blue, 'Heavenly Blue', 'Album' white

Cultivation and uses: good subjects for sunny pockets in the rock garden and for planting at the edges of sunny beds and borders

Phlox
Phlox

Site: sunny

Soil: rich, well drained

Height: 8 to 30 cm (3 to 12 in)

Spread: 30 to 60 cm (1 to 2 ft)

Flowers: small starry blooms of white, pink, crimson, mauve, magenta, blue and purple

Flowering time: spring and early summer

Planting time: spring

Propagation: take cuttings in summer; divide mature plants in spring

Recommended species: *P. subulata* (photograph) 8 cm (3 in) is the species from which many varieties have been derived; among the best of these are: 'Appleblossom' pink, 'G. F. Wilson' pale blue, 'Temiscaming' rosy red, 'Red Wings' crimson. Other notable species are: *P. amoena*, 10 cm (4 in), lilac pink, leathery leaves; *P. douglasii*, 8 cm (3 in), bluish-pink, and varieties *rosea* pink, 'Snow Queen' white; *P. divaricata*, 30 cm (12 in), lilac

Cultivation and uses: replace the plants every few years when they begin to wear themselves out. The carpeting kinds (that is, all the species mentioned except *P. divaricata*) will become rather gappy after several years

Soapwort
Saponaria

Site: sunny

Soil: ordinary, well drained

Height: 15 cm (6 in)

Spread: up to 1 m (3 ft)

Flowers: pink, star-shaped blooms

Flowering time: summer

Planting time: spring or autumn

Propagation: sow seeds outdoors in spring; take cuttings of healthy young growths in autumn; divide mature plants in spring

Recommended species: *S. ocymoides* (photograph) is the most widely grown rock-garden species; it has bright pink flowers and is also offered in varieties such as 'Bressingham', which is slower-growing and brighter pink

Cultivation and uses: in some circumstances the plants can be short lived and may have to be renewed sooner than expected. Superb on the rock garden or in walls where they can be positioned to cast their stems and flowers downwards for the most spectacular effect

Mossy Saxifrage
Saxifraga

Site: rather shady

Soil: rich, moisture-retentive

Height: 10 to 15 cm (4 to 6 in)

Spread: 30 to 90 cm (1 to 3 ft)

Flowers: star-shaped blooms of yellow, white, pink or crimson carried in clusters on short, wiry stems

Flowering time: spring and summer

Foliage: rather fluffy, pale green leaves packed into soft mats

Planting time: spring

Propagation: divide mature plants in spring

Recommended species: several species go to make up the group of saxifrages which are described as 'mossy'; among the best varieties of these species are: 'Cloth of Gold' white with pale green to yellow foliage, 'Dubarry' crimson, 'Flowers of Sulphur' pale yellow, 'Gaiety' rich pink, 'Triumph' bright red

Cultivation and uses: superbly colourful plants for the front of moist, shady borders and pockets of moisture-retentive soil in the rock garden. They will thrive in sun provided that their roots are not allowed to dry out

Stonecrop

Sedum kamtschaticum

Site: sunny

Soil: ordinary, well drained, even dry

Height: up to 15 cm (6 in)

Spread: up to 40 cm (16 in)

Flowers: orange-yellow

Flowering time: summer

Planting time: spring or autumn

Propagation: sow seeds outdoors in spring; take cuttings in summer; divide mature plants in spring

Recommended species: *S. kamtschaticum* has a form with variegated foliage 'Variegatum' (photograph), its leaves are edged with cream, its flowers are yellow and its seed cases are bright crimson

Cultivation and uses: good for growing in dry patches in the rock garden or a gap in paving; also at the front of dry, sunny borders

Stonecrop

Sedum spurium

Site: sunny

Soil: ordinary, well drained, even dry

Height: up to 8 cm (3 in)

Spread: up to 38 cm (15 in)

Flowers: deep pink

Flowering time: summer

Planting time: spring or autumn

Propagation: sow seeds outdoors in spring; take cuttings in summer; divide mature plants in spring

Recommended species: *S. spurium* has a number of varieties; one excellent one is 'Schorbusser Blut' (photograph) which has rosy-red flowers and bronze-tinted foliage

Cultivation and uses: very useful for dry patches and poor soils; matt-forming evergreen particularly suitable for growing in crevices in paths

Houseleek
Sempervivum

Site: sunny

Soil: light and sandy

Height: 2.5 to 5 cm (1 to 2 in), flowers on taller stems

Spread: 30 to 60 cm (1 to 2 ft)

Flowers: pink or red star-shaped blooms

Flowering time: summer

Foliage: very attractive rosettes of succulent leaves; many are tipped with maroon or are entirely that colour, others have hairy outgrowths

Planting time: spring

Propagation: sow seeds under glass in spring; take cuttings using sturdy young rosettes in summer; divide mature clumps in spring

Recommended species: *S. arachnoideum* (cobweb houseleek) has rosettes covered in silky white hairs, the flowers are pink; *S. tectorum* (photograph) has green rosettes tipped with maroon, the flowers are purplish red; *S. calcaratum* has maroon rosettes and purplish-pink flowers; there are many more worthy species and excellent varieties

Cultivation and uses: sempervivums thrive well on neglect but appreciate a topdressing of leafmould and grit in spring. Plant them in sunny crevices in the rock garden, on walls and in paths; some species will grow well in a mixture of clay and cow manure fastened to house roofs

Thyme
Thymus

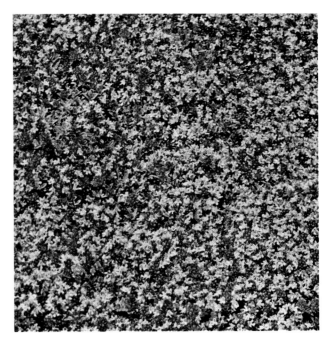

Site: sunny

Soil: light, well drained

Height: up to 30 cm (1 ft) but most are ground-hugging

Spread: up to 1 m (3 ft)

Flowers: tiny hooded blooms of white, pink, crimson, lilac or purple

Flowering time: summer

Foliage: tiny aromatic oval leaves – green, golden or variegated

Planting time: spring or autumn

Propagation: sow seeds outdoors in spring; take cuttings in summer, divide mature plants in spring

Recommended species: *T. citriodorus* (lemon thyme), 10 to 15 cm (4 to 6 in), lilac flowers, and its variety 'Silver Queen' white-edged leaves; *T. drucei*, creeping, purple flowers; *T. vulgaris*, 15 cm (6 in), purple flowers; *T. serpyllum*, creeping, purplish pink, and its many spectacular varieties (photograph).

Cultivation and uses: good carpeters for light soil where they can be used to edge beds and borders. Look well and smell especially fragrant when planted between paving stones where they can be walked on; suitable for sunny pockets and crevices in the rock garden

Aquatic Plants

The great breakthrough in water gardening came, of course, with the introduction of the plastic and glassfibre pools, simplicity itself to fit in position and giving none of the maintenance headaches which are usually associated with concrete constructions – not that there is anything wrong with these provided they are properly made.

With rigid glassfibre pools and plastic or butyl rubber pool liners there is a real need to make sure that the holes they are to go into are made properly with no sharp stones left lying around: with the weight of water bearing down when the pool is filled these can turn into potential wreckers. Also, when positioning one of the rigid-types of pool, make quite sure that it is evenly supported all round; the weight of water will again cause problems if this is not done, this time through distortion of the structure. However, it is a simple matter to make sure that this kind of thing does not occur.

If you decide to have a concrete pool then the sides must be at least 13 cm (5 in) thick and properly waterproofed. One of the great problems with concrete pools is cracking caused by very severe winter weather and, as the plastic and glassfibre kinds can so easily be camouflaged with paved surrounds or marginal plantings, there is every reason for these to be considered a better choice in most home garden conditions.

Planting

Nowadays it is usual to do the planting of aquatics in plastic openwork baskets, rather than in prepared 'beds' of soil on the base of the pools.

When using a planting basket, and these are available in a range of sizes, put a layer of compost (made from good soil mixed with a little chopped-up turf and a handful of bonemeal) in the bottom and around the sides of the basket. Sit the plant on this, pack more compost very firmly over the roots and finish with a layer of gravel to prevent disturbance by fish. If the soil used is on the fine side then a good tip is to line the sides and base of the basket with a piece of sacking.

The basket can then be positioned on the floor of the pool or on one of the ledges if the plant does not need such a depth of water. What you must take heed of is the correct planting depth for the subjects you're dealing with. Water lilies, for instance, vary considerably in their needs; some are suitable for water only 20 cm (8 in) deep, while others grow well in water from about 30 to 60 cm (1 to 2 ft) and still others in water 90 cm (3 ft) or more deep. Advice on the needs of specific varieties of water lilies in this respect is given in the catalogues of nurseries offering these plants, as it is of other aquatics. One of the best and most adaptable of water lilies is the red 'James Brydon' which likes water of medium depth. It is a variety which I would recommend to anyone making a start with water gardening.

Other plants

Oxygenating plants are needed in any pool and especially if you have ornamental fish. These little plants are essential for pool hygiene and for keeping the environment properly balanced. One of the best of these is the water violet, *Hottonia palustris*, which bears whorls of lilac flowers to a height of about 23 cm (9 in) in the early part of summer. *Elodea crispa* is another good choice, also potamogeton and the water milfoil, *Myriophyllum spicatum*. These are planted in baskets as bunches of unrooted cuttings.

Excellent marginal aquatics include *Pontederia cordata* with lavender-blue flowers in summer; the flowering rush, *Butomus umbellatus*; the reed mace *Typha latifolia* and the arrowhead, *Sagittaria sagittifolia*. There are many more, including the kingcup, *Caltha palustris*. These are grown around the edge of the pool in planting pockets of the correct depth. Most appreciate a water depth of about 8 cm (3 in) so if the baskets are about 15 cm (6 in) deep then you will need to provide ledges of around 23 cm (9 in) deep in order to achieve the correct depth.

Bog plants, like the lovely varieties of *Iris kaempferi* and *Gunnera manicata* (if you have room for it) are, of course, grown on the periphery of the pool in wet soil – wetness which is contrived artificially if it isn't naturally occurring.

Yet another group of water plants are the free-floating kinds. The interesting thing about these is that they do not require any anchorage in the soil but simply float in the water.

Once the planting up is completed you should wait a few weeks before introducing any fish. The recommended rate for stocking is to allow 5 to 8 cm (2 to 3 in) of fish for every 30 cm square (1 sq ft) of water surface area.

Pool maintenance

As long as the correct balance of plants, fish and snails is maintained most pools need little regular care. But it is important to remove dead leaves and debris from the surface regularly and for this I find that a wire rake is a good tool.

After several years, you may feel that the plants are overcrowded and this is then a good time to empty out the water (after having carefully removed the fish), divide the plants and give the pool a good cleaning.

In winter, if the water freezes over and remains frozen for more than a week it is necessary to make a hole in the ice to allow any gas given off by decaying vegetation to escape, otherwise it may well poison the fish. Never break the ice with a hammer or heavy object as the shock waves may injure the fish, use a pool heater or pour boiling water on the surface. If using the last method it will probably be necessary to repeat it frequently to keep the hole open.

Pools can be easily made with
plastic or butyl rubber liners. Make
sure that there are no sharp stones
underneath. Glassfibre pools must
be completely level and placed
on a firm base

Planting a water lily
in a basket

Section through a pool to show the
different planting levels

Water Hawthorn

Aponogeton

Type: fixed-floating aquatic

Site: sunny or shady

Water depth: 10 to 45 cm (4 to 18 in)

Flowers: fragrant white, tiered petals and black anthers

Flowering time: summer

Foliage: floating, oval green leaves sometimes spotted with purple

Planting time: late spring or early summer

Propagation: sow seeds as soon as ripe in pots of wet soil; divide mature clumps at planting time

Recommended species: *A. distachyus* (photograph) is the most popular species

Cultivation and uses: valuable plants for both the appearance and scent of their blooms. They can be grown in pools or tubs. Divide and replant every two or three years

Fairy Floating Moss

Azolla

Type: free-floating aquatic

Site: sunny or partially shady

Water depth: unimportant

Foliage: pinkish-green frilly fronds turning bronze-pink as the weather gets colder in autumn

Planting time: transfer to the pond in early summer when danger of frost is past

Propagation: frost-tender, so in cool climates overwinter some plants in a bowl of water in a frost-free greenhouse. Plants reproduce themselves by division

Recommended species: *A. caroliniana* and *A. filiculoides* (photograph) are the best kinds. They are similar in appearance, though *A. filiculoides* has slightly larger fronds

Cultivation and uses: attractive and delicate plants for ponds or tubs. Thin out if the plants grow too quickly

Flowering Rush

Butomus

Type: marginal aquatic

Site: sunny

Water depth: shallow edges of pools

Height: 60 to 120 cm (2 to 4 ft)

Flowers: large round heads of pink star-shaped blooms carried on long stems

Flowering time: summer

Foliage: green, rush-like leaves

Planting time: spring

Propagation: divide mature clumps in spring

Recommended species: *B. umbellatus* is the only species

Cultivation and uses: a colourful waterside plant for pools and lakes. Divide clumps when they become too large

Kingcup

Caltha

Type: marginal aquatic

Site: sunny or partially shady

Water depth: shallow water or muddy soil around edges of pools

Height: 23 to 30 cm (9 to 12 in)

Flowers: large, single or double yellow or white buttercup blooms

Flowering time: spring

Foliage: large, round, deep green leaves

Planting time: spring

Propagation: divide mature clumps after flowering

Recommended species: *C. palustris* (photograph) is the commonest species and it has two excellent varieties in *plena*, double, and *alba*, white. *C. polypetala* is a much larger yellow-flowered kind growing to 60 or 90 cm (2 or 3 ft)

Cultivation and uses: colourful spring-flowering marginals at home in any moist spot and growing well with very little attention. Clumps can be divided when they grow too large

Prickly Rhubarb
Gunnera

Type: bog plant

Site: sunny or partially shady, sheltered

Water depth: prefers to be in moist soil rather than in the water

Height: up to 3 m (10 ft) and even more across

Flowers: 60-cm (2-ft) high greenish-brown heads of flowers

Flowering time: summer

Foliage: enormous rhubarb-like leaves which are usually 120 to 150 cm (4 to 5 ft) across but may be even larger. The stems are green and prickly

Planting time: spring

Propagation: sow seeds under glass in spring; divide mature plants in spring

Recommended species: the commonest and most spectacular species is *G. manicata* (photograph)

Cultivation and uses: the plant must have moisture at all times and enjoys a deep, rich soil. Its leaves will be cut to the ground by the first frosts and the crowns of the plant must be protected with dried leaves and bracken through the winter if they are to survive in cool climates. A bold and eye-catching plant for the larger garden

Yellow Flag
Iris

Type: marginal aquatic

Site: sunny or partially shady

Water depth: shallow edges of pools and lakes

Height: 60 to 90 cm (2 to 3 ft)

Flowers: yellow blooms in the classical iris shape

Flowering time: early summer

Foliage: erect sword-like leaves

Planting time: spring or autumn

Propagation: divide mature clumps after flowering

Recommended species: the flag iris is *I. pseudacorus* (photograph). It is available in several varieties including 'Golden Queen', with larger, brighter flowers, and *variegata* which has leaves striped with creamy white

Cultivation and uses: attractive, natural-looking plants for the margins of pools and lakes. Divide the clumps when they become too large

Japanese Iris
Iris

Type: bog plant

Site: sunny

Water depth: will grow either in moist, lime-free soil surrounding the pool or in good earth in shallow water

Height: 60 cm (2 ft)

Flowers: purple, blue, lilac, pink and red blooms of the classical iris shape, except that the 'fall' petals are held almost horizontal. This has resulted in the plant being called the 'clematis-flowered iris'

Flowering time: summer

Foliage: green, sword-like leaves

Planting time: spring or autumn

Propagation: divide mature clumps after flowering

Recommended species: the Japanese Iris is *I. kaempferi* (photograph) which is available in a number of named varieties in the shades indicated above

Cultivation and uses: extremely attractive plants for the margins of pools and the sides of streams. Divide the clumps when they become too large

Duckweed
Lemna

Type: free-floating aquatic

Site: sunny or partially shady

Water depth: unimportant

Foliage: little round discs of green

Planting time: introduce to the pool in spring

Propagation: the plants increase themselves by division

Recommended species: there are several duckweeds in common cultivation and the following are among the most popular: *L. minor*, small-leaved, very common; *L. gibba* (photograph), the thick duckweed; *L. trisulca*, ivy-leaved duckweed, oval fronds which grow at right angles to one another, submerged (except in summer when it rises to the surface)

Cultivation and uses: once introduced to a garden pond duckweed will need no encouragement to thrive. Indeed, it will need thinning out if it is not to cover the surface completely. However, it provides shade and food for fish and makes a pleasing green mosaic on the water if its spread can be limited

Bog Bean

Menyanthes

Type: marginal aquatic

Site: sunny or partially shady

Water depth: shallow edges of pools, streams and lakes

Height: a few inches above water level

Flowers: white blooms, tinged with pink, carried on stiff stems

Flowering time: early summer

Foliage: oval green leaves carried in threes

Planting time: spring

Propagation: divide mature clumps in spring and replant pieces of stem with a few roots attached

Recommended species: *M. trifoliata* (photograph) is the best and most frequently grown type

Cultivation and uses: will grow in moist and boggy ground as well as shallow water. Lift and thin out when clumps become too large

Monkey Flower

Mimulus

Type: marginal aquatic

Site: sunny or partially shady

Water depth: shallow edges of pools, streams and lakes, or moist, boggy soil

Height: 15 to 45 cm (6 to 18 in)

Flowers: orange, red or yellow trumpets (often contrastingly spotted)

Flowering time: summer

Foliage: fresh green leaves carried right up the stems

Planting time: spring

Propagation: sow seeds under glass in spring; take cuttings of healthy young growths and root in a propagator in summer

Recommended species: *M. luteus* (syn. *M. guttatus*), 30 to 45 cm (12 to 18 in), yellow spotted with red; *M. ringens*, 45 cm (18 in), lilac-purple, small-flowered. There are many hybrids with variously coloured flowers including: 'Bees' Dazzler', 15 cm (6 in), red; 'Orange King' (photograph), 15 cm (6 in), orange and yellow, and 'Whitecroft Scarlet', 15 cm (6 in), bright red

Cultivation and uses: these are plants that bring vivid colour to the waterside but they are rather short lived and should be renewed each year from seeds or cuttings to make sure of their survival

Water Forget-me-not
Myosotis

Type: marginal aquatic

Site: partially shady

Water depth: shallow edges of pools, streams and lakes, or moist, boggy soil

Height: 23 to 30 cm (9 to 12 in)

Flowers: small, round, pale blue blooms

Flowering time: early summer

Foliage: pale green, oval leaves

Planting time: early spring

Propagation: sow seeds outdoors in spring; divide mature colonies in spring

Recommended species: the water forget-me-not is *M. palustris* (syn. *M. scorpioides*)

Cultivation and uses: superbly decorative plants for the water's edge where their misty blue flowers will be carried in profusion

Water Lily
Nymphaea

Type: fixed-floating aquatic

Site: sunny

Water depth: about 15 to 45 cm (6 to 18 in)

Flowers: large, open, lotus-like blooms of white, red, pink or yellow, often pleasantly scented

Flowering time: summer

Foliage: large green plate-like leaves float on the surface of the water

Planting time: spring

Propagation: by division of mature plants in spring

Recommended species: *N. alba* is the white water lily native to Britain but it is rather too vigorous for all but the largest pool or lake. The following hybrids give a good show of bloom: 'Gladstoniana' white; 'Marliacea Chromatella' yellow; 'Mrs Richmond' deep pink; 'Escarboucle' wine red; 'James Brydon' crimson. For very small pools and tubs where the water is shallow *N. odorata minor* is a superb, scented, white-flowered species that is happy in from 10 to 23 cm (4 to 9 in) water

Cultivation and uses: excellent where there is sufficient water surface for them to spread without becoming a nuisance. Replant them in their baskets every two years or so. Flowers can be picked when young and placed in bowls of water indoors

Water Fringe
Nymphoides

Type: fixed-floating aquatic

Site: sunny or partially shady

Water depth: 15 to 45 cm (6 to 18 in)

Flowers: wide open blooms with fringed petals of white or yellow

Flowering time: summer

Foliage: green, heart-shaped leaves

Planting time: spring

Propagation: divide mature clumps in spring

Recommended species: *N. indica*, (water snowflake) white with a yellow centre; *N. peltatum* (photograph), yellow

Cultivation and uses: divide and replant when clumps become too vigorous. Very decorative in pools and tubs

Close up of nymphoides flower

Pickerel Weed
Pontederia

Type: marginal aquatic

Site: sunny

Height: 45 to 60 cm (18 to 24 in)

Water depth: boggy soil or shallow water up to 15 cm (6 in) deep

Flowers: spikes of lavender-blue blooms

Flowering time: summer

Foliage: green leaves the shape of arrow-heads, carried on sturdy stalks

Planting time: spring or early summer

Propagation: divide mature clumps in spring

Recommended species: the species most commonly grown is *P. cordata* (photograph). Its variety *lancifolia* has longer leaves

Cultivation and uses: plant either in boggy soil at the water's edge or in a basket just beneath the surface of the water. A very decorative plant

Arrowhead
Sagittaria

Type: marginal aquatic

Site: sunny

Water depth: shallow edges of pools and lakes

Height: 30 to 45 cm (12 to 18 in)

Flowers: three-petalled or double blooms of white

Flowering time: summer

Foliage: large green leaves the shape of arrow-heads

Planting time: spring

Propagation: divide mature clumps in late spring

Recommended species: *S. sagittifolia* is the single-flowered form and its variety *flore pleno* the double-flowered variety

Cultivation and uses: divide and thin out when clumps become too large. Excellent plants for foliage effect and the flowers are most attractive in the double form

Reed Mace
Typha

Type: marginal aquatic

Site: sunny or partially shady

Water depth: shallow edges of pools and lakes or boggy ground

Height: 1 to 2 m (3 to 6 ft)

Flowers: dark brown 'pokers' which eventually turn white and fluffy

Flowering time: summer

Foliage: large, green, grassy leaves

Planting time: spring

Propagation: sow seeds in a wet mixture of peat and sand in spring; divide mature clumps in spring

Recommended species: *T. latifolia* (photograph) is the true reed mace (often wrongly called bulrush). Smaller and less rampant species are *T. angustifolia*, 1 to 1.25 m (3 to 4 ft) and *T. minima*, 30 to 45 cm (12 to 18 in)

Cultivation and uses: for the larger species you will need plenty of room and thinning out will be necessary when clumps become overcrowded. The flower heads can be cut and dried for winter decoration

Index to Botanical Names

Index to Common Names